HANDBOOK

of

BASEBALL DRILLS

HANDBOOK

of

BASEBALL DRILLS

Archie P. Allen

Baseball Coach, Springfield College

PRENTICE-HALL, INC.

Englewood Cliffs, N.J.

PRINTED IN THE UNITED STATES OF AMERICA

37418

PREFACE

HANDBOOK OF BASEBALL DRILLS PRESENTS OVER 200 drills including variations for every situation that confronts a coach in developing individual players and molding them into an effective team. These drills can be performed in the gym early in the season or out-of-doors, as the situation allows.

Outdoor practice sessions need not be dull affairs with half of the team being inactive. The coach should plan his practice sessions so that each player is active in some phase of his particular specialty. It is important that drills be varied, not drawn out, and executed with enthusiasm. Little time is needed to explain a drill; this can be done in the gym during early practice. Team morale depends greatly upon interesting practice sessions and keeping everybody busy.

Drills will aid in developing players' confidence and poise. The more a skill is repeated, the surer a player becomes in his performance. Many players who are not naturals in their positions have to be developed. Repetition through various types of drills teaches them to perform skills more automatically and naturally.

While the various phases of practice are taking place, players unconsciously condition themselves physically and mentally. In many instances a coach can condition a player despite the player's attitude toward hard physical work, merely through interesting and motivating drills.

Through drills, the coach can more accurately evaluate a player's ability, coordination, and coachability. At the same time, a player is more apt to realize his shortcomings and is thereby in a position to accept the coach's final selection of team personnel.

The two practice drills outlines which conclude this book serve as a guide to more productive daily practice and total teaching.

Archie P. Allen

CONTENTS

Chapter 1

Conditioning Drills

BECAUSE THERE IS A DEFINITE CORRELATION BETWEEN strength and performance, the smart coach employs a set of drills which, if executed conscientiously, develop a player's physical strength as well as his mental alertness. This effort takes discipline, and a well-disciplined player is a coach's dream.

A physically conditioned player will progress more rapidly to game conditions and situations than one who tires and has to ease up. It is impossible to be alert, energetic, and well-coordinated if one is not up to the level of conditioning required of a good performer. Thus, preparation of players physically should be stressed in your conditioning phase of pre-season work.

The physical condition of a player depends largely on himself and his attitude toward participation in baseball. As coach you can set down all types of conditioning drills, but if the player does not have the drive to work industriously at them he is selling himself short as well as the team. Lip service is not enough. Concentrated work is as much required in this phase of team preparation as it is on the field during regular practice sessions.

A player who can discipline himself to work hard on his own, or in the company of another player, is one who can be depended upon to get the job done during the competitive season. There is no substitute for hard work, and getting oneself into proper physical condition is hard work. The old axiom "You play just like you practice" is never more true than in this phase of team preparation. A player can't loaf during practice and expect to be an outstanding performer during the game.

The following drills build a player physically to ready him for the practice sessions and the season ahead. These drills are varied so there will be something adequate for any type of facilities at hand. Lack of proper facilities is no excuse for not having an adequate physical conditioning program.

PRE-SEASON INDOORS

1. Weight training drill for throwing and hitting

Weight lifting is frowned on by many because it has the implication of one becoming muscle bound, but it is harmless if it is intelligently controlled.

This drill develops wrist and forearm muscles. This should aid greatly in snap of throw as well as getting more distance in hitting.

Procedure: Wrist snap (both wrists)

(a) Grasp a small barbell (5 lbs.)
(b) Rest elbow on firm support.

Drill No. 1 A

(c) Keep forearm vertical.
(d) Snap wrist forward and backward.

Drill No. 1 B

Wrist curling (both wrists)

(a) Use barbell, elbow and forearm as above.
(b) Rotate wrists in both directions.
(c) Make larger circles each time.

2. All-around weight training

This drill gives an all-around strength conditioning to the player. This should be done three days a week with basketball or handball activity in between.

Procedure:

(a) Clean (weights at rest at shoulder level, arms flexed) and press; 10 repetitions, light weight.

(b) Alternate press with dumbbells, pressing one while lowering other 10 times, two sets.

(c) Hop jump, five repetitions, four sets, 30 lb. weight.

(d) Light pull over, 10 repetitions, after each hop jump set.

(e) Sit up with weight behind head, twisting to touch elbows to opposite knees, alternately 10 repetitions.

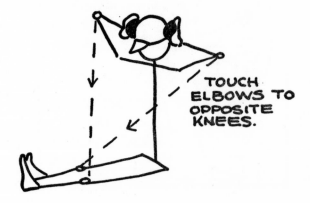

(f) Supine press, 10 repetitions.

(g) Straight arm lateral raise, 10 repetitions.

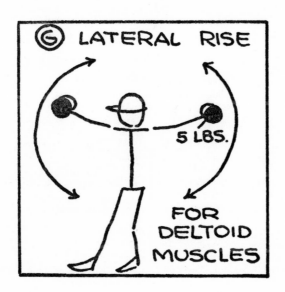

(h) Throwing motion using pulley weight, 20 to 30 throws.

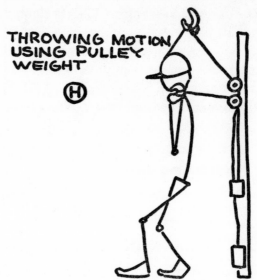

THROWING MOTION USING PULLEY WEIGHT (H)

(i) Swing a bat and throw after each session.

3. Team conditioning drill

This drill builds strength and endurance. All these exercises are based upon speed, interval training, and the overload principles.

Procedure:

(a) Push ups—30 seconds (on finger tips).
(b) Sit ups—2 minutes—as fast as possible.
(c) Spot run—10 innings—an inning consists of running in place for 10 seconds and then resting 10 seconds.
(d) Squat jumps—30 seconds—as fast as possible.

Use these exercises after a regular practice.

4. Handball

Handball helps develop a baseball player's keen eye,

shiftiness of foot, ability to stay close to the ground, and hand-eye coordination; it also takes off surplus weight. Everything done in baseball is done in handball.

Handball can be played the year around but should be intensive, for a month or so, three times a week until the concentrated outdoor practice begins. Pitchers should discontinue when they begin throwing hard in the early season. Continued handball may harm their work on control.

5. Leg conditioning drill

This drill develops stamina in the legs for running speed, quick starts, and endurance.

Procedure:

(a) Players work independently or in pairs.
(b) Take start position similar to track runner.
(c) Sprint 30 yards, slow down and walk 30 yards.
(d) Repeat several times, increasing number daily.
(e) Finish off with a run for distance; increase distance daily.

6. Indian club drill

This drill increases flexibility of the shoulder area, strengthens the fingers, wrists, and forearms, and, with repetition, builds endurance. Excellent for pitchers.

A. Exercise for shoulders: Arm circles sideward, outward and inward; also forward and backward, outward and inward.

B. Exercise for forearms and elbows: Elbow circles sideward, outward and inward; also forward and backward.

C. Exercise for wrists: Wrist circles sideward, outward and inward; also forward, backward and horizontal above and below.

Procedure for each exercise:

(a) Single circles sideward.
   1. Four outward right arm.
   2. Four outward left arm.

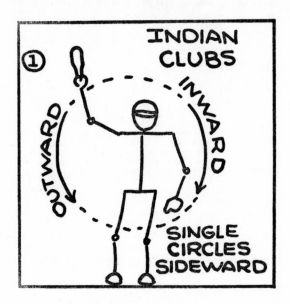

   3. Four inward right arm.
   4. Four inward left arm.
(b) Double arm circle
   1. Four outward.
   2. Four inward.
(c) Parallel arm circle
   1. Four outward.
(d) Alternate left and right arm
   1. Four right.
   2. Four left.

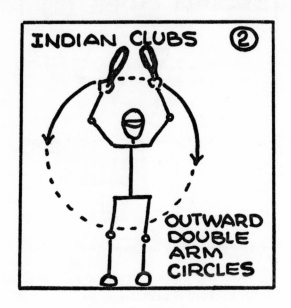

INDIAN CLUBS ②

OUTWARD DOUBLE ARM CIRCLES

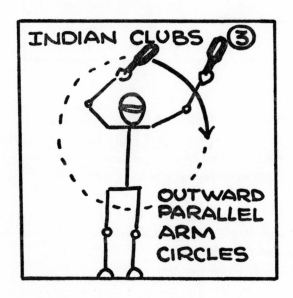

INDIAN CLUBS ③

OUTWARD PARALLEL ARM CIRCLES

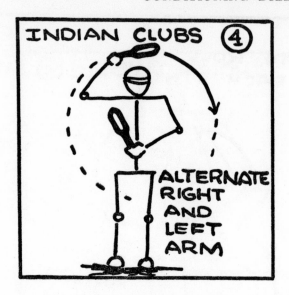

(e) Increase repetitions after several sessions.

(f) These exercises may be worked in combination rather than singularly if desired.

7. Reaction drill

This drill develops reactions in fielding bouncing or ground balls.

Procedure:

(a) Two men face each other three feet apart.

(b) Legs are spread and body is bent at waist.

(c) Bounce, toss or roll ball through other man's legs.

(d) Ball may be caught with either hand (no glove used).

(e) Players may use any fake but may not move feet.

(f) Ball is played continuously until it goes through legs of one of the players.

(g) Keep score for motivation.

Drill No. 7

8. Reaction drill (2)

This drill conditions reflexes and bending, as in fielding a ground ball.

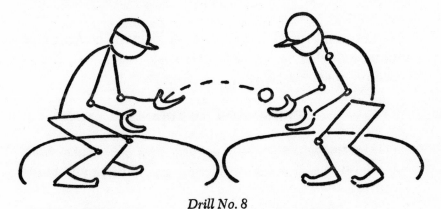

Drill No. 8

Procedure:

(a) Two men face each other.

(b) Each player assumes fielding position and draws circle as far as can reach without moving feet.

(c) The two circles are tangent to each other.

(d) Object is to toss ball over the other player's line in the air without hands crossing center line.

(e) Ball may not be thrown outside the semi-circle.

(f) Players may not move their feet.

(g) Keep score for motivation.

Miscellaneous suggestions for heavy resistance training: Pulley weights, medicine balls, spring tensor grips, climbing ropes, sledge hammer swinging, and squeezing rubber ball.

There is a drill for any type of physical plant that a coach may have at his disposal. Above are several suggested drills that will fit one situation or another. The coach should select the type most fitted for his particular conditions. After each heavy session of calisthenics, weight lifting, Indian clubs, medicine ball, spring tensor grips, a period of running, and reaction drill, the player should swing a bat and throw a ball for a while. Thus the heavy muscle building will be associated with the particular movements that are going to be most used by the player. This will also ensure that as strength develops, performance will naturally maintain its progress proportionately.

PRE-SEASON OUTDOORS

The major portion of the early part of outdoor work should be spent on drills involving conditioning. Drills requiring running, particularly for the pitchers and outfielders, should be stressed during the first week of practice. Accustoming the feet and legs to the wearing of spikes, especially following the indoor period in which sneakers have been used, should be a gradual process.

9. Team conditioning drill (see drill 3, preceding)

The purpose of this drill is to continue to build strength and endurance. It should be continued for at least two weeks. If this drill hasn't been used previously it should be continued for at least a month to prove beneficial.

10. Running drill "A trip"

This drill develops strength, endurance, and wind.

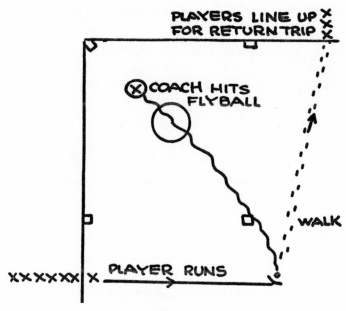

Drill No. 10

Procedure:

(a) Line players on right-field foul line.

(b) On command and in turn each player runs hard to center field, where coach hits a fly ball to be caught on the run.

(c) Ball is caught or retrieved and thrown to coach.

(d) Player continues to jog to left field foul line.

(e) Once over and back constitutes a trip.

(f) Pitchers should take five trips a day.

(g) Infielders and outfielders should take three trips a day.

(h) Drill should continue up to the day of the first game.

11. Pitcher conditioner

This drill maintains and improves the condition of the pitcher and aids in taking off excessive weight.

Procedure:

(a) Pitcher takes his regular turn throwing for batting practice.

(b) Coach takes player to outfield.

(c) Player faces coach about 30 yards away.

(d) Coach has bat and several baseballs, and an assistant who can be a pitcher waiting his turn.

(e) Coach hits short pop flies in all directions. The coach may find that throwing the ball may prove more successful for accuracy.

(f) Pitcher must catch ball in the air and throw it to assistant.

(g) As soon as ball is caught the coach hits another in opposite direction.

(h) Pitcher should catch 25 without a miss.

(i) If ball is missed, one is taken off the number already successfully caught.

(j) Increase number of catches daily.

(k) Shower immediately following drill.

(l) Drill should not be continued as vigorously after season begins.

12. Variation: pitcher conditioner—keeping pitcher active and warm

This drill keeps the pitcher active, warm and in condition during early season.

Procedure:

(a) Warm up for batting practice.

(b) Pitcher waiting turn should play pepper.

(c) Pitch batting practice.

(d) Early in season, it might be advisable to take several turns of twenty pitches.

(e) Follow pitching by hitting fungoes.

(f) Then take relays from outfielders.

(g) During infield practice take several 50-yard sprints.

(h) Finish up with two laps.

(i) Shower.

COMPETITIVE SEASON

After the season is in full swing, it is necessary to maintain the players' condition. This is possible for the infielders and outfielders because their daily training is vigorous enough to keep them at the peak of condition. However, the pitcher's daily work is not so devised, and it is necessary to continue work on his training. As the pitcher goes, so goes the team, and as the season progresses his task becomes more difficult and important to the success of the team.

Chapter 2

Pitching Drills

THERE ARE VARIED OPINIONS AS TO THE PROPER METHOD of readying the pitcher in early season work. However, they are all based on the premise of developing his control and at the same time improving the physical condition of his arm and body. Because of the fact that many coaches have estimated that up to 80 per cent of a baseball team's strength is pitching, it is imperative that you spend sufficient time with your pitching staff.

See to it that the pitcher is adequately educated in the proper fundamentals of his position so that each move or habit is developed into a normal pattern. The normal pattern, fundamental in nature, must never be deviated from, if the pitcher wishes to keep his poise, confidence and control. Among the following drills are those which will aid a great deal in preparing the pitcher's physical condition, control, mental alertness, coordination, and know-how about his position. The pitcher should work with the catcher who is going to catch him as often as he can, and spend half of each session pitching from a stretch. Everything that is done outdoors can also be done in the gym, except a full-scale game.

PITCHER WORKING WITH CATCHER INDOORS

13. Conditioning pitcher's arm

This drill conditions the pitcher's arm during early workouts. Pitchers should be throwing at least a month before first game.

Procedure:

(a) Use a regulation home plate, a cardboard painted white or a home plate painted on a rubber mat.

(b) Regulation pitcher's plate or one painted on rubber mat should be used.

(c) Use two pitchers to one catcher.

(d) Pitchers throw easily from about 30 feet.

(e) After they are sufficiently warm they move back to 45 feet.

(f) Pitchers throw ¾ speed only, working on form and control.

(g) Toward latter part of workout they should spin the ball a few times, not vigorously—just enough to get the feel of it.

(h) When arm feels a little tired workout should stop.

(i) Repeat this ¾ speed at 45 feet for a week.

14. Pitching form

This drill develops the habit of stepping directly toward home on pitcher's stride and follow through.

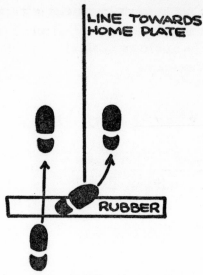

Drill No. 14

Procedure:

(a) Use regulation home plate and pitcher's rubber or one that has been painted on the floor or on a rubber mat.

(b) Draw a line from the middle of the pitcher's rubber toward center of home plate.

(c) Pitcher must step to the outside of this line on his stride.

(d) Striding foot must land on the ball of the foot.

(e) Check for overstriding, for direction of the step, and for landing on the ball of the foot.

15. Pitcher's control

This drill aids a pitcher's control.

Procedure:

(a) Following the usual warm-up period the catcher calls out ball or strike.

(b) Manager records the catcher's decisions.

(c) Records are posted on bulletin board daily.

16. Control variations

This drill sharpens a pitcher's aim.

Procedure:

(a) Use catcher's glove as a target.

(b) Catcher calls for high, low, inside or outside pitches.

(c) Use catcher's knee or shoulders for a target when pitching inside or outside, high and low.

(d) Catcher should indicate with his glove where he wants the ball and then hold target in middle of the plate.

(e) Pitchers should never throw the ball over middle of the plate.

17. Pitching-control practice with "strings"

This drill develops control.

Procedure:

(a) By using strings a strike zone can be made, simulating a batter standing at the plate to bat.

(b) Strings are set over the plate with the catcher situated in his regular catching position.

(c) Pitcher delivers the ball to various spots as designated by the catcher.

(d) It is very easy to see how accurate the control is.

(e) Keep a daily record of successful strikes out of 50 pitches.

Procedure in making the "strings":

(a) Use high jump or volleyball standards if in the gym.

(b) The posts or standards should be far enough apart to allow a batter to stand in his regular position.

(c) String used is heavy cord; light cord or twine will break.

(d) Upper string is tied at armpit level.

(e) Lower string is tied at knee level.

(f) The two vertical strings are tied the width of home plate.

(g) Ball hitting string will not deflect dangerously.

(h) A set of strings should be standard equipment at the practice field for daily use by all pitchers.

18. Pitching control with strings (variation)

This drill teaches the pitcher to keep the ball low.

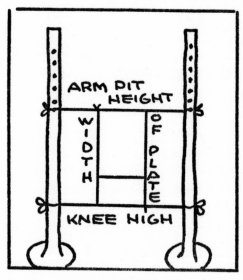

Drill No. 18

Procedure:

(a) Use the above string setup.

(b) Place another string about a third of the way up.

(c) Object is for the pitcher to put the ball in this smaller area.

(d) Keep a record of successes.

19. Pitcher follow-through drill

This drill teaches pitchers to follow through on all pitches.

Procedure:

(a) Pitcher loosens up his arm as usual by throwing easily, and gradually increasing intensity.

(b) Pitcher while throwing hard must pick up grass, stone or stick after each pitch, then replace it.

(c) Repeat this daily until follow through becomes a habit.

(d) Pitcher continually throwing high is usually in too upright a position; he must bend over.

20. Pitcher throwing to bases

This drill helps to practice form and the throw to first baseman, second baseman, shortstop and third baseman.

Procedure:

(a) Use pitcher, catcher, one infielder.

(b) Pitcher works with first baseman until technique is established.

(c) Use other infielders in turn until all bases are covered.

(d) Coach stresses the importance of having a good move to the bases as well as an accurate throw.

(e) Continued work on this phase will be used in the various pick-off drills.

21. Coach's check drill

This drill is a check on the fundamentals of each pitcher to insure that he isn't developing bad pitching habits.

Procedure:

(a) Usually used after several days of early season practice.
(b) Pitcher warms up for about 10 minutes.
(c) Reports to the coach ready to throw hard.
(d) Coach checks form.
(e) Coach watches each type of pitch to see if all are thrown the same.
(f) Coach checks hiding the ball.
(g) Coach checks technique of holding man on base.
(h) Coach checks on proper form in throwing to bases.
(i) Coach observes everything the pitcher does and makes corrections and suggestions.

22. Pitcher fielding bunts

This drill teaches the pitcher to field a bunted ball.

Procedure:

(a) A pitcher, catcher and fielder are needed.
(b) Pitcher throws to catcher, catcher rolls ball down first or third base line.
(c) Pitcher fields ball while catcher makes call, and throws to first base.
(d) Move fielder to second base and repeat procedure.

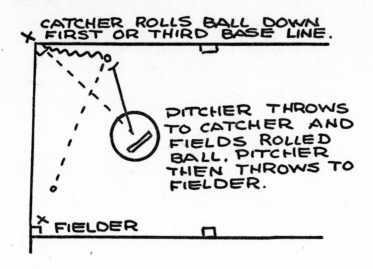

Drill No. 22

(e) Move fielder to third base and repeat procedure.

(f) Finally, pitcher must toss underhand to the catcher on a squeeze play.

23. Pitcher covering home on a passed ball

This drill teaches the pitcher the proper way to cover home plate on a passed ball or wild pitch.

Procedure:

(a) Use all pitchers and catchers.

(b) Pitcher pitches to home and catcher rolls ball behind him.

(c) Pitcher covers home and receives a throw from the catcher.

(d) Coach stresses proper fundamentals on covering home on this play.

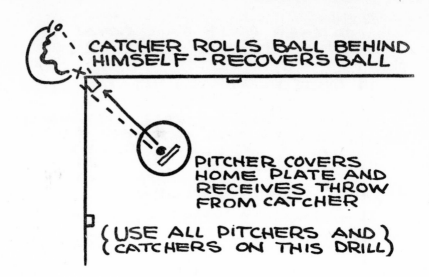

CATCHER ROLLS BALL BEHIND HIMSELF — RECOVERS BALL

PITCHER COVERS HOME PLATE AND RECEIVES THROW FROM CATCHER

(USE ALL PITCHERS AND CATCHERS ON THIS DRILL)

Drill No. 23

PITCHER WORKING WITH FIRST BASEMAN

24. Pitcher covering first base

This drill teaches the fundamentals of the pitcher covering first base on a ball hit to the first baseman.

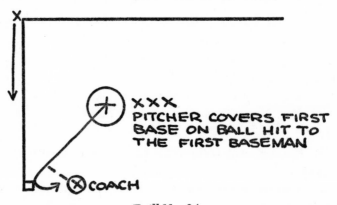

PITCHER COVERS FIRST BASE ON BALL HIT TO THE FIRST BASEMAN

COACH

Drill No. 24

Procedure:

(a) Pitchers line up one behind the other at pitching plate.

(b) In turn each breaks in an arc for first base after making motion of pitching and following through.

(c) Coach tosses the ball to each pitcher, stressing the proper fundamentals.

25. Pitcher covering first base

This drill teaches the pitcher how to cover first base and how to receive the ball from the first baseman.

Procedure:

(a) Use catcher, pitcher and first baseman.

(b) Pitcher pitches to the catcher in *good* form.

(c) Catcher rolls the ball to the first baseman.

(d) Pitcher breaks in an arc for first and takes a toss from the first baseman.

(e) Catcher should break to back up the play at first.

26. Pitcher covering first and taking a long throw

This drill teaches the fundamentals of the pitcher covering first on a ball hit deep or between first and second where a long throw either by the second baseman or first baseman is required.

Procedure:

(a) Line pitchers up at mound.

(b) In turn, on command, pitcher breaks directly for first base.

(c) Coach throws the ball directly over the base.

(d) Coach stresses fundamentals involved.

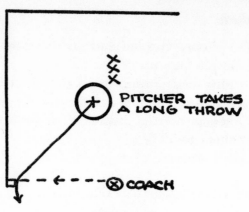

Drill No. 26

27. Pitcher covering first base on long throw from second baseman or first baseman

The purpose of this drill is to teach the pitcher to cover first base properly and receive the long throw from the first baseman.

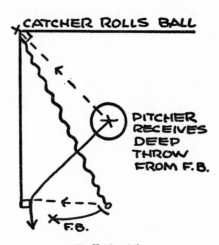

Drill No. 27

Procedure:

(a) Use pitcher, catcher and first baseman.

(b) Line pitchers up at mound.

(c) In turn they pitch in good form and the catcher rolls the ball deep to the first baseman.

(d) First baseman throws ball directly to the base.

(e) Pitcher breaks directly for the base.

(f) Coach stresses fundamentals involved.

28. Pitcher covering first (variation)

This drill teaches the pitcher and first baseman to work together on a batted ball to the first baseman.

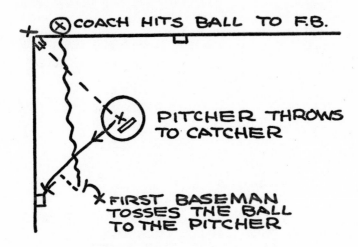

Drill No. 28

Procedure:

(a) Use a pitcher, catcher and first baseman.

(b) Pitcher pitches to the catcher in good form.

(c) Coach hits ball to the first baseman.

(d) Pitcher covers first according to where the ball is hit.

(e) First baseman should always throw or toss to the pitcher for the practice even if ball is near base.

(f) Use runners as a variation.

29. Pitcher and first baseman working together on a ground ball

This drill coordinates the play on a ball that either the pitcher or the first baseman can field.

Procedure:

(a) Pitcher on the mound.

(b) Pitcher pitches to the catcher in good form.

(c) Coach hits the ball out of his hand between the pitcher and first baseman. Catcher may roll ball as a variation to learn the technique.

(d) Pitcher calls, "I have it" if he can field the ball.

(e) First baseman covers first base.

(f) Pitcher continues on to first if he cannot make the play and receives a toss or throw from the first baseman.

(g) Repeat often.

(h) Use runners as a variation.

30. Pick-off drill

This drill teaches the pitcher to pick off a runner and gives practice in pitching form with runner on first base.

Procedure:

(a) Use all the pitchers, a catcher, a first baseman and a base runner.

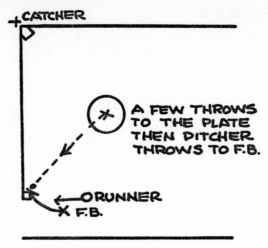

Drill No. 30

(b) Pitcher stretches and assumes his pitching set position on the rubber.

(c) Pitcher can see both batter and, by peripheral vision, the first baseman and the runner.

(d) Pitcher throws a few pitches to the plate.

(e) Using same motion, he completes a throw to the first baseman.

(f) Vary the throw to the baseman, using ¾ speed most of the time.

(g) Then practice a quick snap throw.

(h) Coach stresses fundamentals of pitching with runner on first, and the pitcher's move to first base.

31. Pick-off drill—variation I

This drill helps to pick the runner off first base from a stretch position.

Procedure:

(a) Use all the pitchers, catcher, first baseman and base runners.

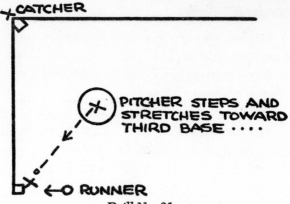

Drill No. 31

(b) Pitcher steps and stretches toward third base line, paying no attention to runner.

(c) Pitcher comes set and looks to first.

(d) Pitcher then makes his pitch to home plate.

(e) Continue this for several pitches so that the impression of the move is complete.

(f) After the impression is complete, pick the runner off base by a quick throw anytime during the stretch.

(g) Coach should be at the mound explaining theory and technique.

32. Pick-off drill—variation II

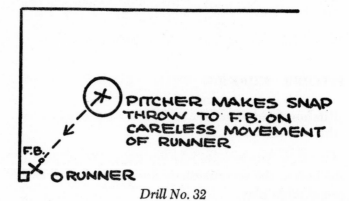

Drill No. 32

Procedure:

(a) Pitcher places right foot on rubber with left foot in front and pointed slightly toward home plate.

(b) Pitcher stretches directly overhead watching runner out of the corner of his eye.

(c) Pitcher brings arms down slowly to set position.

(d) Pitcher makes a quick snap throw to first baseman on any careless move by the runner.

(e) Coach should be at the mound explaining theory and technique.

33. Pick-off at first base when not holding runner on base

This drill develops timing between the pitcher and first baseman on picking the runner off first base when he is not being held on the base.

Procedure:

(a) Use all the pitchers, a catcher, a first baseman and a runner.

(b) Pitcher takes his pitching position.

(c) Pitcher doesn't particularly seem concerned about the runner.

(d) On prearranged signal the pitcher turns and makes a quick throw to first baseman covering the base.

PITCHER WORKING WITH SECOND BASEMAN

34. Pitcher fielding a batted ball and throwing to the second baseman

This drill teaches the techniques of the pitcher throwing the ball to the second baseman in an attempt at a force out or a double play.

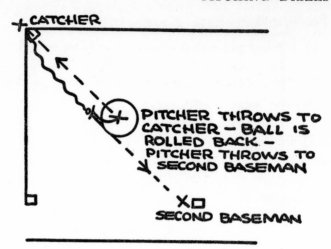

Drill No. 34

Procedure:

(a) Use all the pitchers, a catcher and a second baseman.

(b) Pitcher pitches from stretch position in good form to the catcher.

(c) Catcher rolls ball back to pitcher.

(b) Pitcher fields the ball, pivots, and throws to second baseman for force out.

(e) Second baseman practices footwork of the double play without throwing ball.

Variation, room permitting:

(a) Add a first baseman and a base runner at home.

(b) Second baseman executes the double play.

35. Pick-off drill

This drill teaches the technique of picking off a runner at second base. Usually a right hand hitter.

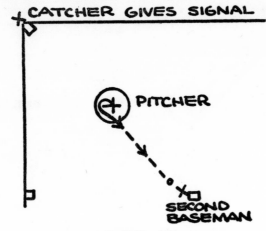

Drill No. 35

Procedure:

(a) Use all the pitchers, a catcher and a second base-man.

(b) Pitcher assumes his normal pitching position, with a runner on second base.

(c) Pitcher throws to the catcher occasionally to practice pitching form with man on second.

(d) On a given signal the pitcher pivots and throws to the second baseman.

(e) Coach stresses the pitcher's pivot and the spot where he wants the ball thrown.

Variation: Use a runner to simulate game conditions.

PITCHER WORKING WITH SHORTSTOP

36. Pitcher fielding a batted ball and throwing to shortstop

This drill teaches the technique of the pitcher throwing the ball to the shortstop in an attempt at a force out and a double play.

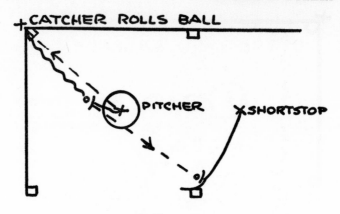

Drill No. 36

Procedure:

(a) Use all the pitchers, a catcher and a shortstop.

(b) Pitcher assumes his normal pitching position with a runner on first base.

(c) Pitcher pitches in good form.

(d) Catcher rolls the ball back to the pitcher.

(e) Pitcher pivots and throws to the shortstop covering second.

(f) Shortstop foots the bag for a double play but doesn't throw the ball.

Variation:

(a) Use a first baseman and base runners at first base and home.

(b) Shortstop executes the double play.

37. Pick-off drill

This drill teaches the technique of the pick-off play at second base with the shortstop.

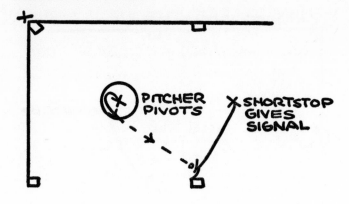

KEY

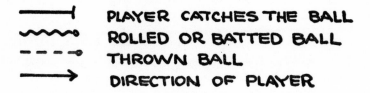

PLAYER CATCHES THE BALL
ROLLED OR BATTED BALL
THROWN BALL
DIRECTION OF PLAYER

Drill No. 37

Procedure:

(a) Use all the pitchers, a catcher and a shortstop.

(b) Pitcher assumes his normal position with a runner on second.

(c) Pitcher throws to catcher occasionally to practice his form with a runner on second.

(d) On a given signal from the shortstop, the pitcher pivots and throws to the shortstop.

(e) Coach stresses fundamentals of the pivot and spot where the ball should be thrown.

Variation: Use a runner to simulate game conditions.

PITCHER WORKING WITH THIRD BASEMAN

38. Fielding a bunted ball down third base line

This drill teaches the fundamentals involved on a bunt with a runner on second base.

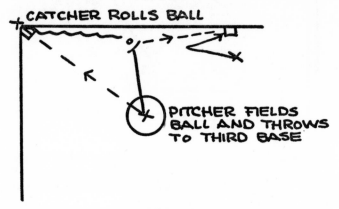

Drill No. 38

Procedure:

(a) Use all the pitchers, a catcher, a third baseman and a first baseman.

(b) Pitcher pitches from his normal pitching position with a runner on second.

(c) Catcher rolls the ball down third base line.

(d) Pitcher calls "I have it" and third baseman returns to third for the throw.

(e) If the ball goes by the pitcher, the third baseman will make the throw to first base.

Variation:

(a) Use a batter and allow him to bunt the ball down the third base line.

(b) Catcher should wear full gear.

39. Pick-off drill at third base

This drill is a practice of the fundamentals of the pick-off of a runner on third.

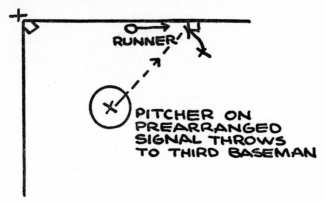

RUNNER

PITCHER ON
PREARRANGED
SIGNAL THROWS
TO THIRD BASEMAN

Drill No. 39

Procedure:

(a) Use all the pitchers, a catcher and a third baseman.

(b) Pitcher assumes a normal position on the mound holding a runner on base.

(c) On a prearranged signal the pitcher makes a quick throw to the third baseman.

(d) Third baseman breaks for the base and receives the throw from the pitcher.

(e) Coach stresses the fundamentals of the movements of the pitcher in executing the play.

Variation:

(a) Use a runner at third base who assumes a lead off the base at various distances.

(b) Pitcher learns to throw with a man on base and at the same time learns to recognize when a runner has too long a lead.

PRE-SEASON OUTDOORS

The same drills that have been used indoors may be used outdoors. The pitcher should now take his regular turn at pitching batting practice. While pitching batting practice, control is to be emphasized. The base on balls by the pitcher is one of the biggest problems confronting a coach.

40. Control drill

This drill teaches the pitcher control by pitching to the batter in various positions and stances in the batter's box.

Procedure:

(a) Use pitcher, catcher and batter.

(b) Pitcher strives for control by aiming at a part of the catcher's body.

(c) Pitcher never looks at the batter.

(d) Batter does not strike at ball; he observes and calls ball or strike.

(e) Batter assumes different positions and stance in the batter's box with each pitch.

41. Base runner drill

This drill teaches the pitcher to remain calm and gain poise with runners on base.

Procedure:

(a) Use pitcher, catcher, batter and a complete infield.

(b) Runner on first jumps around, makes plenty of noise, and tries to rattle the pitcher.

(c) Pitcher pitches to catcher when it is evident that the runner isn't going anywhere.

(d) Continue this until pitcher learns to be calm.

(e) Place runner on second base and repeat same procedure at second base.

(f) Place runner on third base and repeat same procedure at third base.

42. Pitcher fielding bunts

This drill helps to perfect the technique of fielding a bunt under game conditions. Infielders get practice on their technique as well as batter in his bunting fundamentals.

Procedure:

(a) Use a complete infield with catcher in full gear.

(b) Batters bunt and run to first base.

(c) Pitcher throws ¾ speed for strikes.

(d) Pitchers must field every bunt.

(e) First baseman and third baseman field bunt only if the ball is bunted too hard.

(f) Catcher continues to make all calls to first base.

(g) Repeat this drill and make all throws to second base.

(h) Repeat and make all throws to third base.

(i) Repeat and toss home as in a squeeze play.

43. Intra-squad game

This drill is designed to work the pitcher continuously under strenuous game conditions.

Procedure:

(a) Put one team on the field.

(b) The team at bat remains at bat until three and a half innings, or nine outs, have been completed.

(c) As soon as three men have been retired another inning begins.

(d) If offensive team has men on bases when the third out is made, they go to the bench and a new inning begins with none out for the team at bat.

(e) This allows pitcher to work continuously for three full innings.

(f) After his turn as a pitcher is complete, he immediately takes a shower.

(g) Another pitcher takes his position in the box.

44. Two-and-one baseball

This drill teaches the pitcher the importance of the next pitch, builds confidence in throwing curves and other pitches, and develops know-how in pitching in the clutch.

Procedure:

(a) Two teams play an intra-squad game.

(b) Each batter will go to bat with a count of two balls and one strike on him.

(c) Three outs constitute half an inning, or one team may bat as long as a coach desires.

(d) Pitcher gets more experience because he faces more batters.

COMPETITIVE SEASON

During the competitive season the pitcher must take a regular turn at pitching to batters in batting practice. He should also pitch to a catcher each day to work on his control and special pitches. The day before a game the pitcher should throw hard for a short period, taper off, and go to the showers.

Chapter 3

Catching Drills

Next to pitching, catching is the most important position on the team and yet it is in nature an unattractive position to young ball players. The catcher is the quarterback of the baseball team; he sees and directs a large part of the defensive play. Therefore, he must be reliable and be able to instill confidence in the team. The catcher must also be well trained to coordinate his feet, arms and body smoothly.

PRE-SEASON INDOORS

45. Catching-fundamentals drill

The purpose of this drill is to teach the catcher the proper methods of giving signals, giving a target, position of bare hand and catching stance.

Procedure:

(a) Catchers face coach.

(b) Coach demonstrates fundamentals.

(c) Catchers on command from the coach assume stance for giving signal.

(d) On second command catchers assume stance for receiving the ball, giving target and placing the bare hand in the proper position.

(e) Repeat until all have reasonably good form.

(f) Catchers should practice these fundamentals daily while warming up pitchers.

46. Forward-step drill

The purpose of this drill is to teach the proper method of stepping when receiving pitched balls.

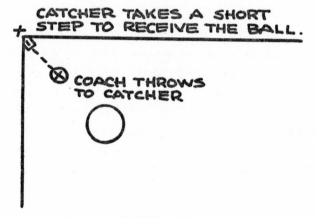

Drill No. 46

Procedure:

(a) Coach takes a position 10 or 12 feet in front of catcher.

(b) Catcher assumes catching position.

(c) Coach tosses ball directly toward catcher.

(d) Catcher takes a short step to receive the ball.

(e) Repeat until movement is learned.

(f) Repeat same procedure to the right and then to the left.

(g) Catcher should practice on his own to master the technique.

47. Throwing drill

The purpose of this drill is to teach the catcher the proper method of preparing to throw to second base.

Procedure:

(a) Coach takes a position about 30 feet in front of the catcher.

(b) Coach tosses the ball to the catcher.

(c) Catcher steps to meet the ball.

(d) On catching the ball he brings glove to the shoulder of his throwing hand.

(e) Throws ball overhand to the coach.

(f) Repeat until coach is satisfied that the fundamental is understood.

(g) To master, catcher should repeat this continually while warming up the pitchers.

48. Gripping-the-ball drill

The purpose of this drill is to teach a catcher to grip the ball in preparation for a throw.

Procedure:

(a) Catcher tosses ball in the air four or five feet.

(b) Grip ball as soon as it comes into the glove.

(c) Learn to grip the ball cleanly and quickly.

(d) Assume throwing position immediately.

49. Balls-in-the-dirt drill

The purpose of this drill is to teach the catcher to catch or block balls in the dirt.

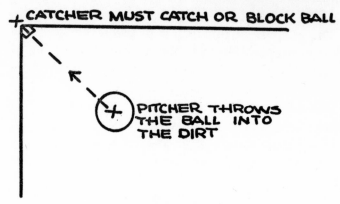

Drill No. 49

Procedure:

(a) Catcher assumes catching position in full gear.

(b) Coach throwing from the mound throws the ball into the ground in front of the catcher.

(c) Catcher attempts to catch the ball cleanly or block it.

(d) Ball should be thrown to the right and left as well as in front.

(e) Coach stresses fundamentals.

50. Return throw to pitcher

The purpose of this drill is to teach the catcher to throw accurately to the pitcher.

Procedure:

(a) Coach should explain the principle at first workout.

(b) During daily warm-up periods and team drills the catcher should fix a spot on the pitcher's chest and try to hit it.

(c) Mastery of this fundamental will be less tiring on the pitcher.

51. Footwork of catcher

The purpose of this drill is to teach the footwork of a catcher in preparation to throwing to a base.

Procedure:

(a) Line catchers up about six feet apart facing the coach.

(b) Coach stands about 20 feet away.

(c) At designated commands of "low out," "low in," "high out," "high in," "in the dirt," or "down the middle," the catcher executes desired footwork.

(d) Catcher should assume good throwing position after execution of command.

(e) Repeat until desired fundamentals are thoroughly familiar to the catcher.

(f) Coach finally throws ball to each catcher in turn.

52. Throwing to the bases

The purpose of this drill is to learn and practice the catcher's throw to the bases.

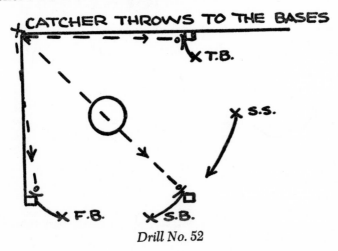

Drill No. 52

Procedure:

(a) Use pitcher, catcher, infielders and a batter.
(b) Pitcher pitches and catcher throws to first base.
(c) Repeat on throws to second base.
(d) Repeat on throws to third base; throw should be over the right hand batter's head.
(e) Proper fundamentals should be stressed by the coach.

Variations:

(a) Place runners on base.
(b) Throw to first attempting to pick runner off base.
(c) Throw to second on attempted steal, runner need not slide.
(d) Throw to third on attempted steal of third.
(e) Throw to third on pick-off attempts.
(f) Use right-handed and left-handed batters.
(g) Various throws on a first-and-third double steal situation.

53. Catching a runner between bases

The purpose of this drill is to teach the technique of putting a runner out who has been caught between bases.

Procedure:

(a) Use pitcher, catcher, infielders, batter and base runner.
(b) Pitcher pitches from a stretch.
(c) Runner moves off base too far.
(d) Catcher cocks his arm and runs directly at the runner.
(e) Putout is made at base farthest from home.
(f) Repeat between second and third base.

(g) Repeat between home and third base.

(h) Coach stresses fundamentals of the play.

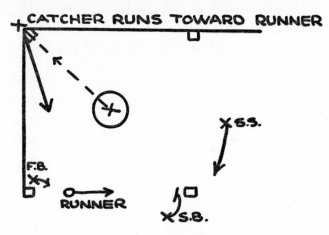

Drill No. 53

54. Catcher fielding a bunted ball

The purpose of this drill is to teach the catcher the proper method of fielding a bunted ball.

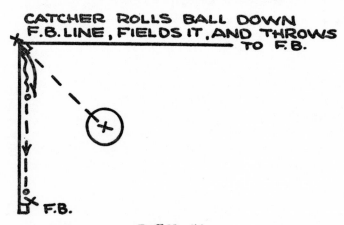

Drill No. 54

Procedure:

(a) Use catcher, pitcher and first baseman.

(b) Pitcher pitches, and catcher catches the ball and rolls it down first base line.

(c) Catcher follows ball, fields it, and throws to first base.

(d) Repeat down third base line.

(e) Continue drill throwing to second base and then to third base.

(f) Coach stresses scooping up the ball and throwing accurately to the bases.

55. Catcher receiving a thrown ball

The purpose of this drill is to teach the fundamentals of taking a throw from various fielders on a play where a runner is trying to score.

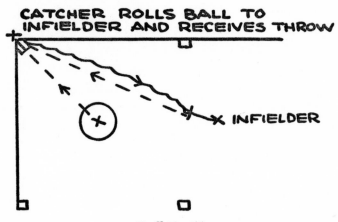

Drill No. 55

Procedure:

(a) Use pitcher, catcher and infielders.

(b) Pitcher pitches and catcher rolls the ball to various positions.

(c) Coach calls the play situation.

(d) Plays to be covered are forceout with the bases loaded and the throw to first for the double play; runner trying to score on an infield hit; and the squeeze.

PRE-SEASON OUTDOORS

The pre-season indoor drills should be repeated outdoors to adjust to outdoor conditions.

56. Pop fly drill

The purpose of this drill is to teach and to practice the catcher catching pop flies. Best place for this is in the outfield so as not to interfere with other work going on.

Procedure:

(a) Use several catchers in full gear.

(b) Catchers take turns.

(c) Catcher assumes catching position.

(d) Coach hits ball from his hand directly overhead.

(e) Catcher catches the ball and returns it to the coach.

(f) Coach stresses pivot, removing mask, getting under the ball, and proper method of catching the ball.

(g) Continue this practice daily as this is one of the most difficult plays a catcher must make.

COMPETITIVE SEASON

There are few specific drills for the catcher. However, the daily workouts with the pitcher, infielders and batters will cover most of the fundamentals concerned with the art of catching. The catcher must discipline himself to hard work and a thorough understanding and knowledge of the fundamentals of his position.

Chapter 4

First Baseman Drills

THE FIRST BASEMAN'S PRIME JOB IS THAT OF CATCHING
a thrown ball. There is hardly a ball hit to the infield that
doesn't ultimately end up at first base. The first baseman
must have a good pair of flexible hands to catch any type
throw. He must be able to shift quickly for bad throws
and leap for high throws. Most professional first basemen
have not always been first basemen but have been taught
to play the position adequately by constant drilling of a
few fundamentals.

PRE-SEASON INDOORS

57. Drill for shifting feet and catching thrown balls

The purpose of this drill is to teach a first baseman to
catch any type of thrown ball.

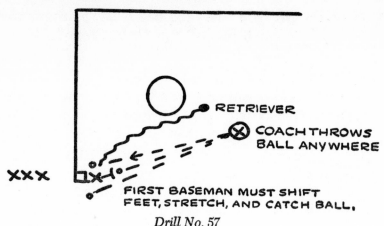

RETRIEVER

COACH THROWS
BALL ANYWHERE

XXX

FIRST BASEMAN MUST SHIFT
FEET, STRETCH, AND CATCH BALL.

Drill No. 57

Procedure:

(a) Coach demonstrates and explains the method of shifting the feet, stretching, and catching the ball.

(b) Prospective first basemen line up at first base foul line.

(c) Each in turn assumes his position to receive a ball from an infielder.

(d) Coach throws several balls to one side, until the shifting is perfected.

(e) Repeat procedure to opposite side.

(f) Repeat procedure on direct throws.

(g) Repeat procedure on balls thrown in the dirt.

(h) Coach repeats procedure and throws the ball so that it pulls first baseman off the base.

(i) Coach then throws ball anyplace, and first baseman shifts his feet accordingly to catch the ball.

(j) This drill should be continued in daily workouts with the first baseman shifting on every thrown ball.

58. First baseman covering first base

The purpose of this drill is to teach the first baseman

to break for first base when the ball is hit, find the base,
and prepare to catch the ball thrown by the infielder.

Procedure:

(a) First baseman in deep fielding position.

(b) Infielders line up one behind the other.

(c) Pitcher or captain hits ground balls to infielder,
who fields the ball and throws it to the first baseman covering the base.

(d) Infielder takes position at end of line after fielding the ball.

(e) Coach is stationed at first base where he stresses
fundamentals and makes corrections.

59. Holding runner on and receiving throw from pitcher

The purpose of this drill is to accustom the first baseman to the various pitching moves of the pitcher and to
practice receiving the throw from the pitcher and tagging
the runner.

Procedure:

(a) Use pitcher, catcher and first baseman.

(b) First baseman assumes position holding a runner on base.

(c) Pitcher makes his various throws to the first
baseman.

(d) First baseman should attempt a tag on imaginary
runner.

Variation:

Use a runner and simulate game conditions of picking off the runner.

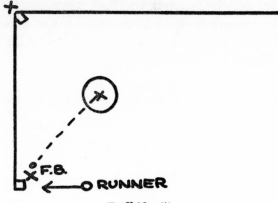

Drill No. 59

60. Fielding a ground ball and throwing

Purpose of this drill is to develop the fielding and throwing to second base by the first baseman.

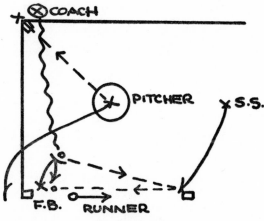

Drill No. 60

Procedure:

(a) Shortstop, pitcher, catcher, and first baseman.

(b) First baseman holds runner on base.

(c) When pitcher pitches, first baseman breaks off the base to prepare to field a ball hit his way.

(d) Coach rolls or bats a ball to the first baseman.

(e) First baseman fields ball and throws to second base.

(f) He returns to first base for return throw.

(g) Coach stresses fundamentals.

61. Fielding a bunt

The purpose of this drill is to teach and practice the fielding of a bunted ball, also to develop teamwork between pitcher, catcher, and first baseman.

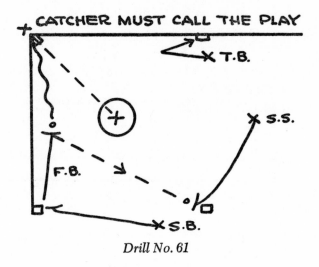

Drill No. 61

Procedure:

(a) Catcher, pitcher and infielders are used.

(b) Pitcher pitches from a stretch.

(c) First baseman holds runner on base.

(d) Catcher rolls ball toward first baseman.

(e) Catcher calls the play as first baseman fields ball.

(f) First baseman throws to proper base as called by catcher.

Variation:

Use a batter to bunt the ball, for more realism.

62. Work with pitcher covering first base

Purpose of this drill is to teach the first baseman the proper method of tossing or throwing the ball to the pitcher.

Procedure:

(a) Repeat drill as used by pitcher covering first base.
(b) Emphasis is on the fundamentals of the toss or throw by the baseman.

63. Taking throws from the catcher

The purpose of this drill is to teach the first basemen the various positions to assume on balls thrown by the catcher.

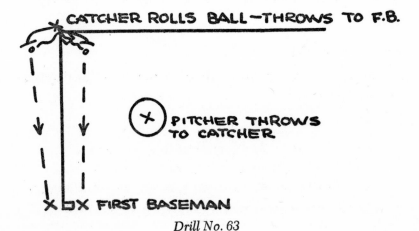

Drill No. 63

Procedure:

(a) Pitcher, catcher and first baseman are used.

(b) Pitcher pitches to the catcher.

(c) Catcher drops ball intentionally behind himself, retrieves the ball, and throws to the outside of first base.

(d) Procedure is repeated but ball is dropped out in front of home plate, catcher retrieves the ball and throws it to the inside of first base.

(e) Catcher signals for a pick-off attempt and, after the pitch, throws it to the base.

(f) These three positions for taking throws from the catcher should be practiced while holding a runner on base as well as with the fielder playing in a position off the base.

PRE-SEASON OUTDOORS

The drills that have been used indoors should now be repeated outdoors continually under game conditions, combining several drills into one. However, the fundamental drills may be omitted unless necessary due to inadequate mastery by an individual. It may be necessary to start again from the beginning with this particular player.

64. Pop fly drill

The purpose of this drill is to practice the catching of pop flies.

Procedure:

(a) Station all first basemen in a line at first base.

(b) Coach hits pop flies to each player in turn.

(c) Coach stresses territory coverage, fundamentals of getting to the ball, and what to do after catching the ball.

(d) Coach may have to call first basemen out for an early practice, because this drill is time consuming and should be done at first base to familiarize the player with field conditions.

COMPETITIVE SEASON

During the competitive season the first baseman should strive to improve on his weaknesses and continue to practice his fundamentals thoroughly. Conscientious hard work will pay off in performance.

Chapter 5

Second Baseman Drills

THE SECOND BASEMAN, WITH THE SHORTSTOP, IS THE backbone of the infield defense. He must be quick, fast of foot, and able to throw from any position. He also must react quickly to bad throws, and catch pop flies all around him. Many hours of constant drilling and practice are required for this all-important position. A team weak at second base cannot be a strong team.

PRE-SEASON INDOORS

65. Fielding and throwing to first base

The purpose of this drill is to get practice at the various positions from which a second baseman must throw to retire the runner at first base.

Procedure:

(a) A catcher is needed to take throws from the first baseman.

72

(b) Line up all second basemen at normal fielding position.

(c) Coach hits ball directly at each fielder who fields ball correctly and throws to first basemen.

(d) Repeat same procedure on balls between fielder and second base, between second baseman and first baseman, and on slowly hit balls just out of the pitcher's reach.

(e) Coach stresses fundamentals of fielding and throwing.

66. Second baseman fielding a slow hit ball

The purpose of this drill is to teach the second baseman to come in fast on a slow hit ball and throw it to the first baseman.

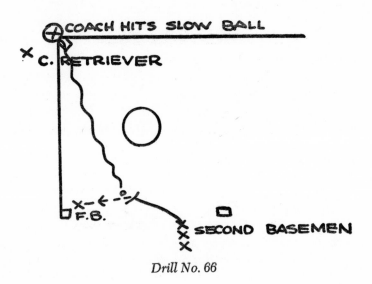

Drill No. 66

Procedure:

(a) Use a catcher to receive throws from the first baseman.

(b) Line up the second basemen at a normal second base position.

(c) Coach rolls or hits the ball slowly to the second baseman.

(d) In turn the second basemen charge in toward the ball, meet it, and field it.

(e) Without straightening up, use a snap throw to the first baseman.

(f) Coach stresses approach to the ball, position on fielding the ball, and the snap throw to the first baseman.

67. Working with first baseman on ground balls

The purpose of this drill is to teach and practice the teamwork involved on a ball that both the first baseman and the second baseman can field.

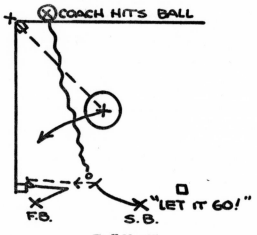

Drill No. 67

Procedure:

(a) Use pitcher, catcher, first baseman and second baseman.

(b) Pitcher pitches in proper form to catcher.

(c) From his hand, coach hits ball between first baseman and second baseman.

(d) Second baseman calls, "Let it go!" and first baseman retreats to first base for the throw.

(e) Pitcher covers first if baseman can't get back.

(f) Coach stresses calling out clearly by the second baseman, and the play of the pitcher and first baseman.

68. Throwing to the shortstop

The purpose of this drill is to practice the proper throws to the shortstop for a double play or forceout.

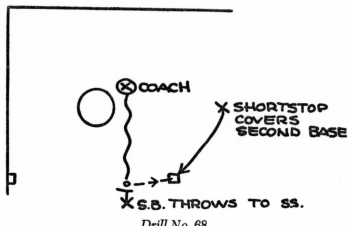

Drill No. 68

Procedure:

(a) Shortstop and second baseman are used.

(b) Coach stations himself in the vicinity of the pitcher's mound.

(c) Coach rolls the ball toward the second baseman who fields the ball and throws to the shortstop at second base.

(d) Repeat to each side and in front until proper

footwork and proper method of making the throw are understood and mastered.

(e) Shortstop doesn't throw the ball, but merely practices his footwork on a double play.

Variation:

(a) After satisfactory results have been obtained in the above drill, the coach hits the ball from home plate.

(b) Coach hits the ball several times to one side of the infielder then the other, until all situations are covered thoroughly.

(c) Balls should not be hit hard, but fast enough to warrant natural performance and to build confidence.

(d) Second baseman cannot waste time on this play; therefore, he should be almost perfect in his actions.

(e) Shortstop shouldn't throw the ball, but practice his approach and footwork.

69. Throwing the ball to home plate

The purpose of this drill is to practice the throw to the catcher after fielding a batted ball.

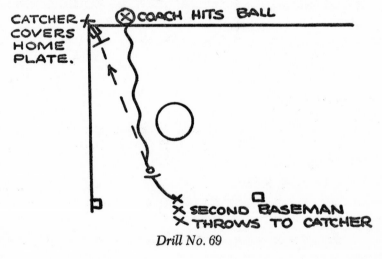

Drill No. 69

Procedure:

(a) Catcher is needed.

(b) Second basemen line up one behind another.

(c) In turn, they move forward to a position nearer home plate than the normal depth.

(d) Coach hits ball to players who field ball and throw it back to the catcher covering home plate.

(e) Coach stresses fundamentals of the throw as well as the work of the catcher in receiving the throw.

70. Receiving throws from pitcher

The purpose of this drill is to practice the timing on the throw from the pitcher after he has fielded a batted ball.

Procedure:

(a) Pitcher, catcher, and first baseman are used.

(b) Pitcher pitches with good form and follows through.

(c) Coach hits a ball back to the pitcher.

(d) Pitcher pivots and throws to second baseman.

(e) Second baseman doesn't throw the ball.

Variation:

(a) Following perfection of the throw, the second baseman foots the base and throws to first for the double play.

(b) Because of the timing element involved and the angle of the throw this play requires a great deal of practice.

71. Pick-off practice

The purpose of this drill is to practice the fundamentals involved in the pick-off play by the second base-man.

Procedure:

(a) Use pitchers and second basemen.

(b) Second basemen line up and take turns covering second.

(c) Pitcher comes to a set position after a stretch.

(d) Pitcher on a signal from the second baseman throws the ball to the second baseman covering the base.

(e) Coach stresses the pivot and the throw by the pitcher and the timing of the play.

Variation:

(a) Use a runner to simulate game conditions.

72. Receiving throw from catcher on a steal

The purpose of this drill is to practice the catcher's throw to the second baseman, and tagging the runner.

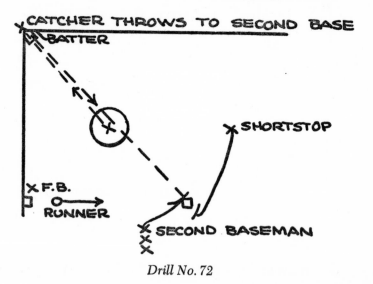

CATCHER THROWS TO SECOND BASE

BATTER

SHORTSTOP

X F.B.
RUNNER

SECOND BASEMAN

Drill No. 72

Procedure:

(a) Use catcher, pitcher and right-handed and left-handed batters who stand in the normal batting position.

(b) Pitcher throws to the catcher.

(c) Catcher steps forward as he catches the ball and throws to second baseman.

(d) Coach alternates catchers so as not to tire their arms.

(e) Coach stresses position on receiving the ball and tagging the runner.

Variation I:

(a) Use a baserunner with the first baseman holding runner on base.

(b) Runner shouldn't slide.

Variation II:

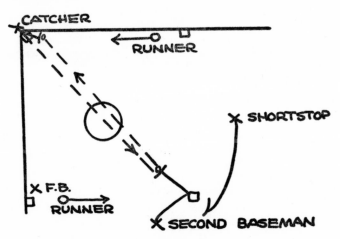

Drill No. 72, Variation II

(a) Runners on first and third.

(b) Runner on first attempts to steal second.

(c) Runner on third breaks for home on throw by the catcher.

(d) Second baseman covers second, charges in to meet the ball and throws home for the putout.

(e) Coach stresses fundamentals of the play.

73. Taking throw from shortstop and making the double play

The purpose of this drill is to practice catching the ball thrown by the shortstop and learning to execute the double play.

Procedure:

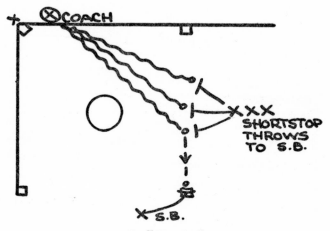

Drill No. 73

(a) Use catcher to aid the coach.

(b) Coach rolls or bats the ball to the shortstop who fields it and throws it to the second baseman covering the base.

(c) Long throws and short tosses should be repeated many times for timing and perfection.

(d) Second baseman foots the base as in a double

play, but doesn't throw the ball to first. He returns it to the catcher.

(e) Coach stresses approach to the base, receiving the ball, and footing the base for the forceout.

Variation:

(a) Repeat same procedure with a first baseman.

(b) Second baseman completes the double play by throwing to first base, practicing various methods of footing the base.

(c) Repeat many times for perfection of the play.

74. Taking the throw from third baseman

The purpose of this drill is to practice taking the long throw from the third baseman, and executing the forceout and then the double play.

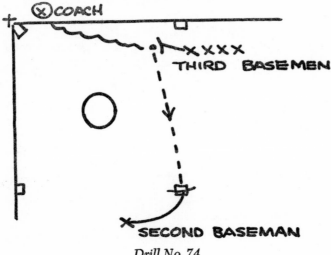

Drill No. 74

Procedure:

(a) Use catcher to aid the coach.

(b) Coach rolls or bats ball to third baseman who fields the ball and makes the throw to the second baseman.

(c) Second baseman takes throw and executes the forceout.

(d) Repeat the footing of the base in executing the double play.

(e) Second baseman doesn't throw the ball to first. He returns it to catcher.

(f) Coach stresses approach to the base, receiving the ball and footing the base.

Variation:

(a) Repeat same procedure using a first baseman.

(b) Second baseman completes the double play.

(c) Repeat many times for perfection of the play.

PRE-SEASON OUTDOORS

All the drills that have been used in the gym should be repeated outdoors continually for perfection of the fundamentals and timing in the execution of various maneuvers. Only through constant drilling can the second baseman effectively carry out the responsibility of his highly important position.

75. Pop fly drill

The purpose of this drill is to teach and practice the catching of pop flies, and to develop teamwork in this area with other players.

Procedure:

(a) Coach will need a manager or catcher to take throws.

(b) Coach hits fly balls behind second base, behind first base, near the pitcher's mound, and directly over the head of the second baseman.

(c) The "Texas Leaguer," or ball hit in between the infielder and the outfielder, should receive a great deal of attention.

(d) Coach stresses territory coverage, sun and wind conditions, calling out "I have it," etc.

76. Second baseman making long throw to home

The purpose of this drill is to teach the second baseman the proper method of throwing to home or third base when he has received a relay from the outfielder or has fielded a ball in short right field.

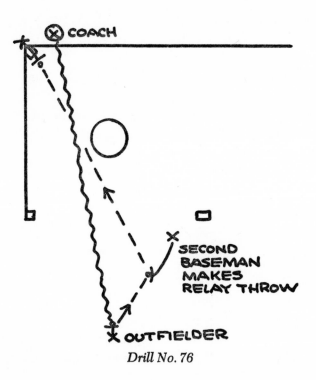

Drill No. 76

Procedure:

(a) Use an outfielder and a catcher.

(b) Coach hits the ball to the outfielder.

(c) Second baseman races to a short right field position and takes a throw from the outfielder.

(d) Second baseman pivots and makes the long throw to home.

(e) Repeat the procedure, throwing to third base.

(f) Coach stresses the fundamentals involved in the play including position in receiving the ball from the outfielder, target offered to the outfielder, and the long throw to home or to third base.

COMPETITIVE SEASON

During this part of the season the second baseman should work continually for perfection in his play at second base. Some one should be hitting grounders to him at every spare moment so that he may practice his fielding and double play work; however, he should not overwork his arm by making too many long hard throws, saving this throwing for the regular infield practice.

Chapter 6

Shortstop Drills

THE SHORTSTOP IS THE MOST IMPORTANT AND THERE-
fore must be the most skillful player in the infield. He
must be a sure fielder, have a very strong arm, be fast afoot,
and be able to throw from any position. Paired with the
second baseman, he is the backbone of the team's defense.
Without a strong second base combination it is impossible
to have a truly championship team. This being the case,
it is imperative that the shortstop be well-qualified to
handle this great responsibility.

The following drills, practiced diligently, will be a
great aid in developing the natural skills that the shortstop
must have.

PRE-SEASON INDOORS

77. Fielding drill

The purpose of this drill is to practice fielding a ball

from the various positions at shortstop. Also, it aids in selection of the most qualified player for the position.

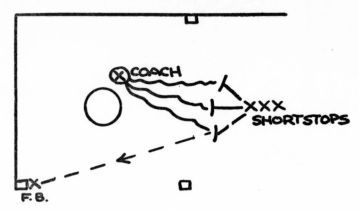

Drill No. 77

Procedure:

(a) Line up shortstop candidates at shortstop position.

(b) Use a first baseman to receive throws.

(c) Coach stations himself about 20 feet in front of the shortstops.

(d) Coach rolls the ball in turn to each of the shortstops.

(e) Shortstop must learn to field the ball hit directly at him, toward second base, toward third, and to take a slow infield hit.

(f) When fielding technique in one direction is mastered, move to another direction.

(g) Coach stresses stance, fielding position, starting, stopping, and throwing.

Variation:

(a) A first baseman and a catcher are needed.

(b) Coach bats the ball from home plate to the

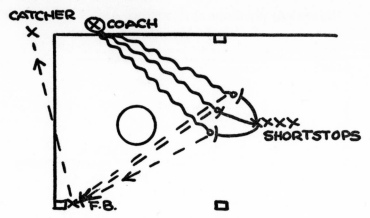

Drill No. 77, Variation

various positions as above, and the shortstop executes his fielding under a more game-like situation.

(c) Coach continues to stress fundamentals.

78. Throwing the ball to second base

The purpose of this drill is to teach the technique of throwing the ball to second base for a forceout or double play.

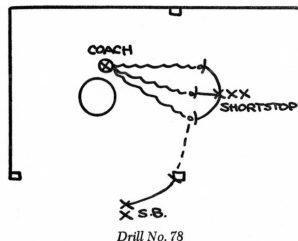

Drill No. 78

Procedure:

(a) Use a second baseman and a catcher to assist the coach.

(b) Shortstops line up at double play depth.

(c) Coach is stationed about twenty feet in front of the shortstops.

(d) Coach rolls the ball toward second base for the toss throw—continue until throw is mastered.

(e) Coach rolls the ball to the third base side for the long throw—continue until mastered.

(f) Repeat by rolling the ball directly at, and then slowly in front of, and then throwing to, second base. Continue until mastered.

(g) Second baseman doesn't throw the ball, he merely catches it and foots the base as in the double play or a forceout.

(h) Coach stresses the importance of getting rid of the ball quickly, and the throw to the second baseman.

Variation I:

(a) Use a first baseman and a catcher.

(b) Coach bats the ball from home plate to the shortstop, and the shortstop executes the type of throw according to where the ball has been fielded.

(c) Second baseman throws to first and completes the double play.

Variation II:

(a) Use baserunner from first base.

(b) Runner should slide on each play.

(c) Second baseman gets practice avoiding runner and varying his style of executing the double play.

79. Receiving throws from second baseman and executing the double play

The purpose of this drill is to teach the approach to second base and the technique of footing the base in executing the double play.

Procedure:

(a) Shortstops line up at double play depth.

(b) On command, in turn, the shortstop approaches second and the coach tosses or throws the ball to the shortstop who foots the base as if executing the double play.

(c) Shortstop doesn't throw the ball.

(d) Continue, only add the throw to first base.

(e) Continue until footwork and approach is mastered.

Variation I:

(a) Repeat procedure and use a first baseman.

(b) Coach rolls the ball to the second baseman who executes the throw to the shortstop.

(c) Shortstop throws the ball to first base for the double play.

(d) Coach stresses approach to the base, technique in executing the double play, and the throw to the first baseman.

Variation II:

(a) Repeat procedure with coach batting the ball.

(b) Use a runner who slides into second base.

(c) Shortstop gets practice executing the double play, getting his throw away, and avoiding the runner.

80. Taking throw from pitcher who has fielded a batted ball

The purpose of this drill is to teach the shortstops to execute a double play on a ball hit to the pitcher.

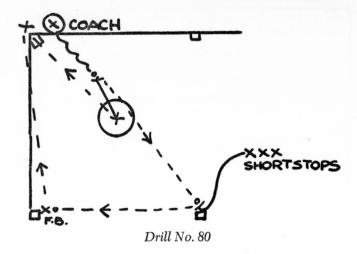

Drill No. 80

Procedure:

(a) Use pitcher, catcher and first baseman.

(b) Coach bats the ball to the pitcher.

(c) Shortstop breaks for second and receives a throw from the pitcher.

(d) Shortstop foots the base and throws to first base.

(e) Coach stresses approach to second, footing the base, and throwing to first base.

81. Pick-off practice

This drill provides practice in the fundamentals involved in the pickoff by the shortstop.

Procedure:

(a) Use pitchers and shortstops.

(b) Shortstops line up and take turns covering second.

(c) Pitcher comes to set position after a stretch.

(d) Pitcher receives a signal from the shortstop.

(e) Pitcher pivots and throws to the shortstop covering second.

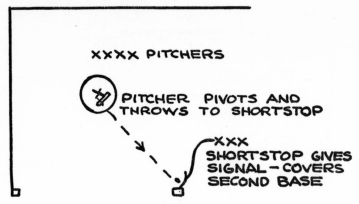

Drill No. 81

(f) Coach stresses timing on the play, the pitcher's pivot, and the shortstop's receiving the throw.

Variation:

(a) Use a runner to simulate game conditions.

82. Receiving catcher's throw

The purpose of this drill is to practice receiving the throw from the catcher on the steal, and on the double steal with men on first and third.

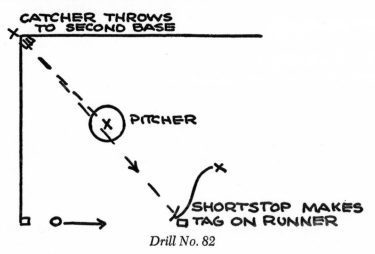

Drill No. 82

Procedure:

(a) Use pitcher, catcher and shortstop.

(b) Pitcher pitches to the catcher.

(c) Catcher steps and throws to second base.

(d) Shortstop positions himself for the throw, catches
the ball, and makes a tag on an imaginary runner.

(e) Coach stresses getting to the base, position at
the base, and tagging the runner.

Variation I:

(a) Use a runner on first base.

(b) Pitcher pitches from a stretch.

(c) Runner shouldn't slide.

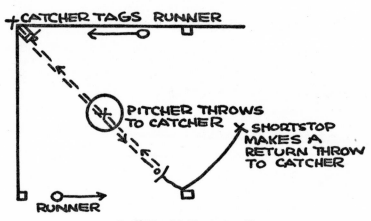

Drill No. 82, Variation II

Variation II:

(a) Runners on first and third are used.

(b) Shortstop races to second for the throw as runner breaks from first.

(c) He moves ahead to meet the ball when runner

on third breaks for home, catches the ball and makes a return throw to the catcher.

(d) Coach stresses techniques of breaking up the double steal.

83. Receiving the throw from the first baseman

The purpose of this drill is to teach the shortstop to take throws from the first baseman.

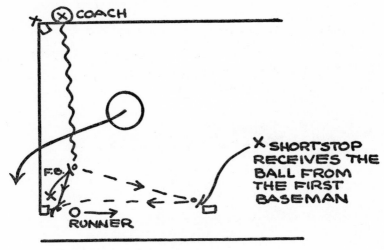

Drill No. 83

Procedure:

(a) Use first baseman and shortstops.

(b) First baseman holds runner on first base.

(c) Coach hits the ball to first baseman who fields the ball in front of the base line between first and second, and throws to the inside of second base.

(d) Shortstop receives the ball and returns throw to first base.

(e) Continue until footwork and approach to second are thoroughly familiar to the shortstop.

(f) First baseman now plays behind the runner at first base and fields the ball behind the base line between first and second base and throws the ball to the outside of second base.

(g) Continue until footwork and approach to second are thoroughly familiar to the shortstop.

(h) Coach stresses the approach to second on a ball fielded behind the runner at first base and the footing of the base in executing this double play.

84. Throwing to home from close infield

The purpose of this drill is to practice the fielding of a ball in close and throwing to home to catch a runner trying to score.

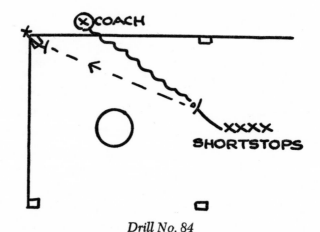

Drill No. 84

Procedure:

(a) Use a catcher and all the shortstops.

(b) Coach hits the ball, a shortstop fields it and throws the ball home.

(c) Coach stresses fundamentals of fielding the ball and the throwing of the ball to the catcher.

PRE-SEASON OUTDOORS

During this phase of practice the various team drills already used indoors should be repeated often to acclimate and adjust to outdoor conditions. During hitting practice, the coach or pitcher should hit grounders continually to the shortstop, who merely fields the ball but doesn't throw to first base. However, half of the time should be spent throwing the ball to the second baseman who goes through the motions of making the double play without throwing the ball to first base. The importance of teamwork between the shortstop and the second baseman is so great that it is impossible for them to get too much practice working together.

85. Catching pop flies

The purpose of this drill is to teach and practice the technique in catching pop flies.

Procedure:

(a) Shortstop assumes his normal position.

(b) Coach hits pop flies behind third base, behind second, in front near the mound, and directly over the head of the shortstop.

(c) Practice on fly balls, "Texas Leaguers," between outfield and infield must be continued constantly.

(d) Coach stresses territory coverage, calling-for-the-ball technique in catching the ball, and adjusting to wind and sun conditions.

86. Shortstop making the long throw to home

The purpose of this drill is to teach and to practice the long throw which the shortstop has to make from short outfield position.

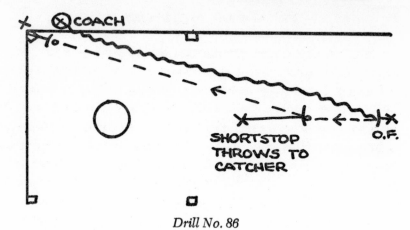

Drill No. 86

Procedure:

(a) Use a catcher and an outfielder.

(b) Coach hits a ball to the outfielder who throws it to the shortstop.

(c) Shortstop pivots and throws to the catcher.

(d) Coach stresses giving a target to the outfielder, and the throw home.

COMPETITIVE SEASON

The shortstop should continually strive to improve his performance through his daily workouts. He, being the most important player in the infield, cannot afford not to work conscientiously at his job.

Chapter 7

Third Baseman Drills

THE THIRD BASEMAN IS THE TYPE OF PLAYER WHO MUST have a great deal of courage, be quick, and have a good arm. His position is one which doesn't call for the many responsibilities and plays that other infielders must make. The ones which he does have to make must be executed perfectly and efficiently; this is possible through a great deal of concentrated effort by the coach and the third baseman. Many third basemen are converted from some other position and need continued work and repetition of the fundamentals of the position.

PRE-SEASON INDOORS

87. Fielding ground balls at third base

The purpose of this drill is to teach and practice catching and throwing the various types of balls that will be hit to the third baseman.

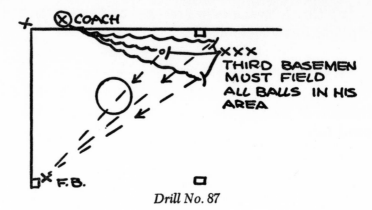

Drill No. 87

Procedure:

(a) Use a first baseman and a catcher.

(b) Line all the third basemen one behind the other in a normal position at third base.

(c) Coach should roll the ball to the third baseman.

(d) The following areas should be covered, each being practiced until the technique is mastered.

 (a) Ball between shortstop and third base.

 (b) Ball between the base and the third baseman.

 (c) Ball directly at the third baseman.

 (d) Ball hit slowly to the third baseman.

 (e) Ball bunted that rolls only a short distance.

(e) Third baseman should field the ball and only lob the ball to a first baseman.

(f) Coach stresses stance, fielding the ball, getting set for the throw, and the throw.

Variation:

(a) Same procedure only coach hits the ball from his hand.

(b) Third baseman may throw harder, but not hard enough to tire the arm.

(c) Coach continues to stress stance, fielding the ball, and proper throwing form.

88. Fielding bunts and throwing

The purpose of this drill is to teach and practice the technique of fielding the bunt and throwing to first or second base.

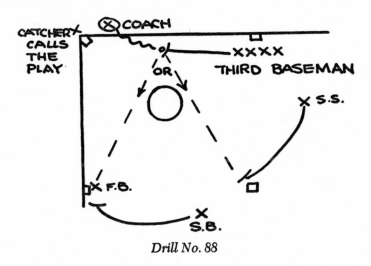

Drill No. 88

Procedure:

(a) Use a catcher, second baseman and shortstop.

(b) Third basemen line up one behind the other in a position on the infield grass anticipating the bunt.

(c) Coach rolls the ball to the third baseman.

(d) Catcher makes the call.

(e) Third baseman fields the ball and throws to the base called by the catcher; second baseman should cover first and shortstop cover second base.

(f) Coach stresses position, stance, fielding the ball, and getting set for the throw.

Variation:

(a) Use a batter who bunts to third base and runs to first.

(b) Use a pitcher who pitches from a stretch, throwing ¾ speed.

(c) Use a runner on first who goes to second on the bunt.

(d) Catcher makes call as usual.

(e) Coach stresses bunting form, as well as third baseman's fielding and throwing the ball.

89. Bunt situation with a runner on second

The purpose of this drill is to teach, practice and coordinate the play of the pitcher and third baseman on a bunt with a runner on second base.

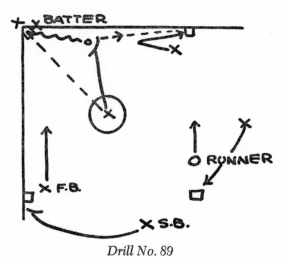

Drill No. 89

Procedure:

(a) Use shortstop who holds runner on base.

(b) Use pitcher who pitches from a stretch throwing ¾ speed.

(c) Use second baseman who takes throw at first base.

(d) Use catcher in full gear.

(e) Batter bunts the ball toward third base.

(f) Pitcher and third baseman move to field the ball.

(g) If pitcher fields the ball, he throws the ball to the third baseman who retreats to the base.

(h) If pitcher can't field the ball, the third baseman continues in, fields the ball and throws it to first base, second baseman covering.

(i) Coach stresses the teamwork between pitcher and third baseman as well as the theory behind the play.

Variations:

(a) Use runner at second who attempts to go to third on bunt.

(b) Batter attempts to beat out the bunt to first.

(c) As a safety procedure, runners shouldn't slide into third.

90. Bunt situation with a runner on third base

The purpose of this drill is to practice putting the runner out on the squeeze play.

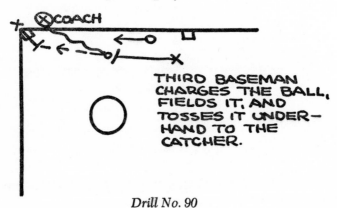

THIRD BASEMAN CHARGES THE BALL, FIELDS IT, AND TOSSES IT UNDER-HAND TO THE CATCHER.

Drill No. 90

Procedure:

(a) Runner on third and a squeeze situation.

(b) Pitcher allows batter to bunt.

(c) Third baseman charges the ball, fields it and tosses it underhand to the catcher.

(d) Runner shouldn't slide.

(e) Coach stresses position, fielding the ball, and tossing the ball to the catcher.

91. Throwing the ball to second base after fielding a batted ball

The purpose of this drill is to teach and practice the technique of throwing the ball to the second baseman for a forceout or a double play.

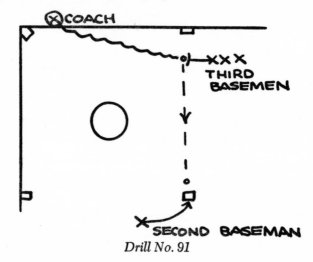

Drill No. 91

Procedure:

(a) Use a second baseman and a catcher to assist the coach.

(b) Third basemen line up in their normal position at third base.

(c) Coach rolls or bats the ball to the third baseman.

(d) Third baseman throws the ball to second base.

(e) Coach stresses accuracy of the throw.

92. Throwing from the base to first base

The purpose of this drill is to teach and practice the throw of the third baseman when he steps on the base for a forceout and then throws to first base for a double play.

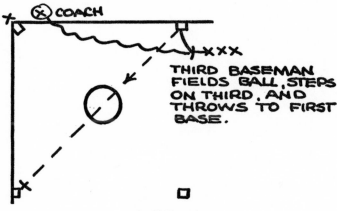

THIRD BASEMAN FIELDS BALL, STEPS ON THIRD, AND THROWS TO FIRST BASE.

Drill No. 92

Procedure:

(a) Use first baseman and catcher.

(b) Coach hits the ball to the third base side of the third baseman.

(c) Third baseman fields the ball, steps on the base and makes the long throw to first base.

(d) Coach stresses tagging the base and throwing the ball.

93. Throwing home after fielding a ball

The purpose of this drill is to practice and master the

technique of throwing the ball home to catch a runner trying to score.

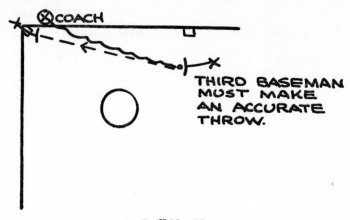

Drill No. 93

Procedure:

(a) Use catcher in full gear.

(b) Coach hits a ball to the third baseman.

(c) Coach stresses good throwing position and taking time to make an accurate throw.

94. Receiving throws from catcher

The purpose of this drill is to teach the position to be assumed at the base, and practice receiving the ball and making a tag on the runner.

Procedure:

(a) Third basemen line up in their normal position at third base.

(b) Pitcher pitches to catcher who throws to the third baseman covering third.

(c) Third baseman takes the throw and makes the tag on an imaginary runner.

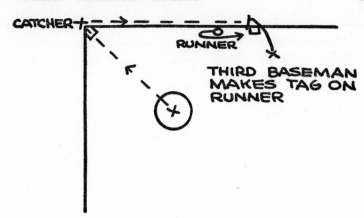

Drill No. 94

(d) After repeating this several times place a runner on third and have the catcher attempt to pick runner off the base.

(e) Coach stresses position of the third baseman in receiving the throw and putting the tag on the runner.

95. Taking throw from first baseman, catcher or pitcher

The purpose of this drill is to practice the technique of taking the throw for a forceout at third.

Procedure:

(a) Coach or player bunts the ball to the various areas in the infield.

(b) All throws are made to third base.

(c) Coach stresses the footwork in taking these throws.

PRE-SEASON OUTDOORS

All the above-mentioned drills that have been used inside can be used to advantage out-of-doors to adjust to outdoor conditions. The third baseman should work hard in everyday practice to perfect his fielding. Many hard-hit balls should be hit to him daily to build his confidence and perfect his technique.

96. Pop fly drill

This drill provides practice in catching pop flies.

Procedure:

(a) Station all third basemen at third base.

(b) Coach in turn hits a fly to each player.

(c) Coach stresses territory coverage, fundamentals of getting to the ball, and what to do after catching the ball.

(d) Coach may call the third basemen out for an early practice. It takes extra work to familiarize the player with the field condition and territory coverage.

COMPETITIVE SEASON

During the competitive season the third baseman should strive to improve on his weaknesses and continue to practice fundamentals thoroughly.

Chapter 8

Outfield Drills

THE OUTFIELDER IS AN IMPORTANT PART OF TEAM DE-fense. He must be alert, fast, have a strong arm, and be skillful in fielding to convert apparent hits into outs and to meet the extra base situation. An outfielder must cover more territory than any other player on the team.

The following drills will develop the outfielder's ability, build his confidence, and impress upon him the important part he has to play in the team's success. The outfield is not a place to put a player just to get him into the lineup unless he has been drilled in the fundamentals involved.

PRE-SEASON INDOORS

97. Catching a fly ball

The purpose of this drill is to teach the proper method of getting to and catching a fly ball.

Procedure:

(a) Line up a group of about eight outfielders facing the coach.

(b) Coach instructs and demonstrates the technique he wants used in catching a fly ball.

(c) Players as a group on "Go" command by the coach reach with hands together for the ball and then allow hands and arms to relax into the body.

(d) Next have them move on "Go" to the side by a crossover step and assume fielding position.

(e) Repeat mimetic drill on balls over the head and to the left.

(f) Repeat mimetic drill on balls over the head and to the right.

(g) Repeat mimetic drill on balls directly over the head where the ball is caught with back to the infield.

(h) Coach stresses getting under the ball, correct position of glove on catching the ball, correct steps in starting for a ball to the side or to the rear, the pivot after catching the ball, and the throw.

Variation:

(a) Used after movements have become familiar and understood by the players.

(b) Coach throws easy fly balls, making the fielders run about 15 feet.

(c) Increase the run depending on the speed of the player and the area being used.

(d) Mastery of these fundamentals is necessary; repeat until they are mastered.

98. Fielding a ground ball

The purpose of this drill is to teach the proper method of fielding a ground ball and then throwing.

1. Pitchers' control will be developed by practice with the strike zone marked off by string. See Drill 17.

2. The pitcher begins his stretch move, looking toward third base and paying no attention to the runner on first. After he comes set, he will check the runner and then pitch. See Drill 31.

3. Another stretch move: The pitcher stretches directly overhead, watching the runner at first from the corner of his eye. He brings his arms slowly down to the set position, and can make a snap throw to first if the runner makes a careless move. See Drill 32.

4. The pitcher should employ this form in gripping the ball. The arm is bent, with the upper arm parallel to the ground and the elbow pointing straight ahead. See Drill 112.

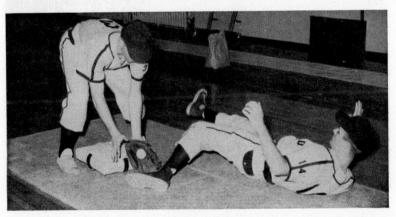

5. An infielder practices tagging a sliding baserunner indoors. See Drill 123.

6. Using the batting "T" indoors, with a mat hung against the wall to minimize bounce. See Drill 149.

7. A timid bunter gains confidence by facing the pitcher and watching the ball all the way from the pitcher's hand to the catcher's glove. He does not attempt to bunt the ball, but merely watches it. See Drill 180.

Procedure:

(a) Again use mimetics to teach these fundamentals.

(b) Coach demonstrates to the group facing him.

(c) On command "Go" the group charges forward about 15 feet and assumes a fielding position.

(d) They field an imaginary ball and simultaneously straighten up and hop into and go through a throwing motion.

(e) Coach stresses approach to the ball, fielding position and method of throwing.

99. Advance work on fielding a ground ball

The purpose of this drill is to practice the fundamentals of an outfielder fielding a ground ball.

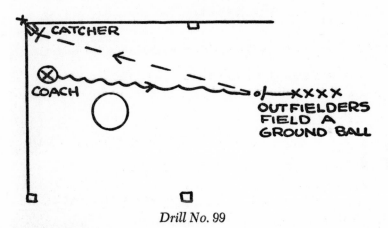

Drill No. 99

Procedure:

(a) Line players one behind the other.

(b) Coach rolls or bats the ball with moderate speed to each in turn.

(c) Players field the ball like an infielder and throw it to a catcher stationed with the coach.

(d) Repeat on balls to the sides as well as directly in front.

(e) This drill should teach confidence as well as technique and should be repeated often.

PRE-SEASON OUTDOORS

The drills used inside with the outfielder have been fewer and less like game situations than those of the other positions. This is due mainly to lack of space. The outfielder, therefore, needs a great deal more work in the practice of his fundamentals than might seem necessary. Someone must be continually hitting the ball to him, so that he can master the techniques that will make him a definite asset to his team. Do not neglect your outfielder; make him feel that he is just as important as any other player.

100. Early season flycatching and throwing practice

The purpose of this drill is to practice catching fly balls and throwing to the bases under outdoor conditions.

Procedure:

(a) Form a semi-circle from left field to right field about twenty yards behind the base line.

(b) Number the players.

(c) The first half throw to third base, the others throw to second.

(d) Keep two balls moving, being careful to place the hits in opposite extremes of the field.

(e) Coach calls out a player's number before the hit.

(f) Later on, call number after the hit.

(g) First balls should be hit easily, gradually increasing the difficulty as practice continues.

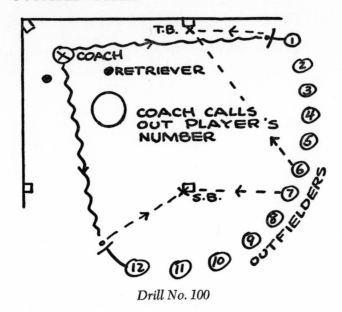

Drill No. 100

(h) Coach stresses stance, approach to the ball, the catch and the throw.

101. Early season grounder practice

The purpose of this drill is to practice fielding the ground ball under outdoor conditions. Fielding ground balls seems to come harder to the beginner than catching fly balls.

Procedure:

(a) Repeat the drill used indoors where players line up in front of the coach and on commands of "Go" practice charging forward and then repeat going sideward to field the ball.

(b) Coach stresses stance, start, approach, and position in fielding the ball.

Variation:

(a) Coach hits the ball at a very moderate speed.

(b) Fielder goes through several easy fielding chances and throws to build confidence.

(c) Increase speed to approach game conditions as nearly as possible.

(d) Coach continues to stress fundamentals.

102. Two-man throwing drill

The purpose of this drill is to practice fielding ground balls and throwing properly.

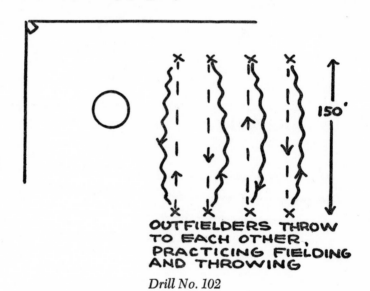

OUTFIELDERS THROW TO EACH OTHER, PRACTICING FIELDING AND THROWING

Drill No. 102

Procedure:

(a) Pair up outfielders.

(b) Place outfielders about 150 feet apart.

(c) They throw to each other, practicing proper techniques of fielding and throwing.

(d) Limit time so as not to tire their arms.

103. Outfield practice in throwing to a relay man

The purpose of this drill is to practice fielding a ball and throwing to a relay man.

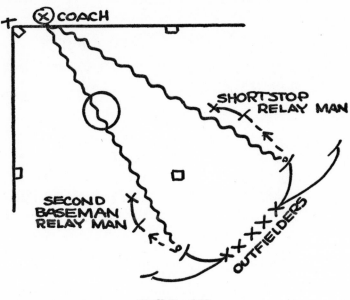

Drill No. 103

Procedure:

(a) Place the group in centerfield and have them take turns fielding the ball.

(b) Player plays the ball as if it were hit under game conditions.

(c) Players should be deep enough so that they must throw to a relay man stationed halfway.

(d) The relay man should be an infielder.

(e) Coach stresses the importance of an accurate throw, throwing with good form, and the target offered by the relay man.

Variation:

(a) Use two balls, two relay men and two catchers to speed up activity and keep practice organized.

(b) Infielders acting as relay men can practice on long one-hop throws to the catcher.

104. Early season outfield starting practice

The purpose of this drill is to develop the habit of starting fast to field a batted ball.

Procedure:

(a) Line players up in the outfield.

(b) Hit grounders for about fifteen minutes and have them charge each one and play it like an infielder.

(c) Then, calling each player in turn, hit the ball to the side so he must pivot and turn to the side in going after the ball.

(d) Next hit the ball directly over the head of the player so that he must turn his back on the ball and run hard to a spot where the ball is expected to land.

(e) Repeat this drill daily until season opens.

(f) Coach stresses stance, pivot, and running after the ball.

105. Catching fly balls in the sun

The purpose of this drill is to practice catching the ball in the sun.

Procedure:

(a) Place all outfielders in the sun field.

(b) Ball may be tossed at the outset to get the feeling of looking into the sun.

(c) Coach then hits pop flies into the sun.

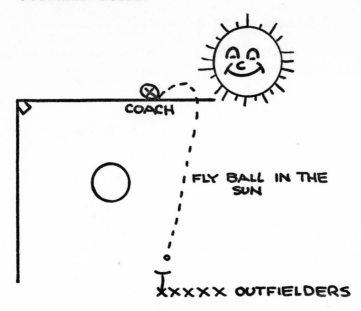

Drill No. 105

(d) Player shields the sun with his gloved hand.

(e) Coach stresses position of the glove, and eyes following the ball into the glove.

Variation:

(a) Use sunglasses and go through the same procedure.

(b) Sunglasses are a part of every team's equipment and some practice with them is required to build confidence in their use.

106. Short-single drill

The purpose of this drill is to practice in throwing to the correct base on the sharply hit single.

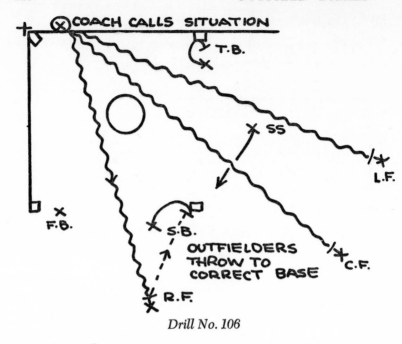

Drill No. 106

Procedure:

(a) Place outfielders in their respective positions straightaway.

(b) Use a complete infield and a catcher.

(c) Coach calls out situation.

(d) Coach hits sharp singles and line drives at each outfielder.

(e) Player charges the ball and throws to the correct base.

(f) Infielders get practice receiving throws at the base from the outfielder.

(g) Coach stresses charging the ball, fielding, throwing, and proper base the ball should be thrown to.

Variation:

(a) Use runners to make drill more realistic.

(b) Runner shouldn't slide.

107. Outfielders' weakness drill

The purpose of this drill is to give practice to over-
come the outfielders' weaknesses.

Procedure:

(a) Line up outfielders one behind the other and
give them plenty of room to run.

(b) Hit to what you think is each player's weakness.

(c) Coach suggests corrections to players.

108. Outfield-fly team practice

The purpose of this drill is to practice the teamwork
involved on a fly ball hit between infielder and outfielder
and between outfielders.

Procedure:

(a) Place infield and outfield in their normal position.

(b) Coach hits fly balls between outfield and infield, so that the infielder must turn his back to the infield
to make the catch.

(c) Outfielder has the right of way and calls for the
ball if he can make the catch.

(d) Next, flies should be hit between the outfielders,
with the proper fielder making the call for the ball.

(e) Coach stresses field coverage and the calling of
"I have it" by the fielder.

COMPETITIVE SEASON

During this season the outfielder should work hard
on his weakness. He must not become careless in his daily
team drills such as relay practice, charging ground balls,
and catching fly balls.

109. Fence drill

The purpose of this drill is to practice fielding a ball that hits a fence in the outfield. Many playing fields are enclosed with a fence, whereas your field may have no fence.

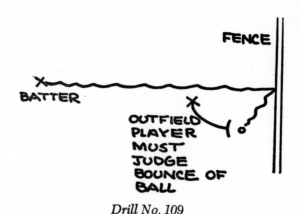

Drill No. 109

Procedure:

(a) During team's batting practice, the outfielders should have an extra pitcher or substitute hit grounders and line drives at the fence.

(b) Outfielders should study actions of the ball very closely.

Chapter 9

Individual Defensive

Fundamentals

A TEAM OF PLAYERS SOUND IN THE FUNDAMENTALS IS hard to beat under pressure and will consistently prove to be in the thick of any game. Championship teams are made up of players well versed in fundamentals. This, however, can be achieved only through constant drilling of the simple techniques.

The following drills are devised to teach a beginner, or one who has definite faults, the most important defensive fundamentals.

110. Gripping the ball

The purpose of this drill is to teach the proper gripping of the ball prior to throwing.

Procedure:

(a) Coach demonstrates and explains the theory.

(b) Players pair up and toss the ball overhand to each other.

(c) Coach stresses correct use of fingers for holding the ball, position in hand and firmness of grip.

111. Throwing drill

The purpose of this drill is to teach the proper method of throwing a ball.

Procedure:

(a) Coach lectures and demonstrates to the group.

(b) Split group up into two lines facing each other about 20 feet apart.

(c) Players throw to each other stressing form.

(d) Increase distance as drill progresses satisfactorily.

(e) Coach stresses stepping, eye on target, overhand throw, leading with elbow, wrist snap and follow through.

112. Arm and wrist drill for a pitcher

The purpose of this drill is to teach the pitcher the movements of his arm and wrist in pitching.

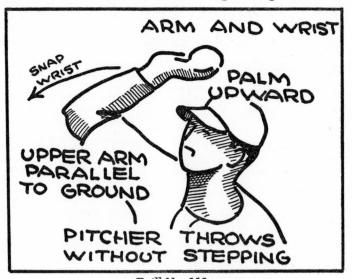

Drill No. 112

Procedure:

(a) Pitchers line up in pairs facing each other about 20 feet apart.

(b) Each pair has a ball.

(c) Pitcher grips the ball for a fast ball and brings the ball over his shoulder, palm upward.

(d) The upper arm is parallel to the ground, bent at the elbow with the elbow pointed directly ahead.

(e) Without stepping, the pitcher throws to his partner straight overhand snapping his wrist downward when releasing the ball.

(f) Repeat the above procedure only this time grip the ball as for a curve and rotate the wrist when throwing.

(g) Repeat procedures and grip ball for the change-up pitch.

(h) Repeat each type of pitch until the pitcher has mastered the fundamentals.

(i) When all pitches are mastered, mix them up, throwing each with same motion of the arm.

(j) Coach stresses grip on the ball, wrist action, leading with the elbow, and throwing all pitches with the same movements.

113. Teaching a player to throw overhand

The purpose of this drill is to teach a player who has a tendency to throw sidearm to throw overhand.

Procedure:

(a) Two players face each other about 20 feet apart kneeling.

(b) Players throw overhand to each other, will be unable to keep their balance if they throw sidearm.

(c) Widen distance gradually.

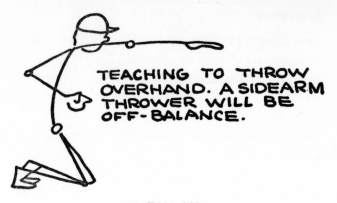

Drill No. 113

(d) Stand and continue throwing practice.

(e) Repeat drill until overhand throw is mastered.

114. Catching a thrown ball

The purpose of this drill is to teach the fundamentals of catching a thrown ball.

Procedure:

(a) Coach lectures and demonstrates to the group.

(b) Split group into two lines facing each other about 20 feet apart.

(c) Players throw back and forth to each other.

(d) Coach stresses stepping to meet the ball, reaching, giving with the ball, using two hands, watching the ball into the glove, gripping the ball, and position of the glove on high and low balls.

115. Catching a fly ball

The purpose of this drill is to teach the correct method of catching a fly ball.

Procedure:

(a) Coach explains and demonstrates to the group.

(b) Coach should toss several fly balls to each to familiarize them with the method of catching the ball.

(c) Coach then pairs the group up and they toss flies to each other.

(d) Coach stresses getting under the ball, position of the glove, and following the ball into the glove.

116. Fielding a ground ball

The purpose of this drill is to teach the technique of fielding a ground ball.

Procedure:

(a) Coach lectures and demonstrates to the group.

(b) Split group into pairs facing each other about 30 feet apart.

(c) Players roll ball to each other, first directly at each other, then to the sides.

(d) Coach stresses going to meet the ball, getting in front of the ball, playing the hop, stop, glove to ground, body low, eye on the ball into the glove, giving with the ball, straightening up, stepping, and throwing overhand.

117. Ground ball practice (variation)

The purpose of this drill is to practice the fundamentals of fielding and throwing a ground ball.

Procedure:

(a) Hang mats on the wall of the gym, or use brick wall as it is.

(b) Infielders line up one behind the other about 30 feet in front of the mats.

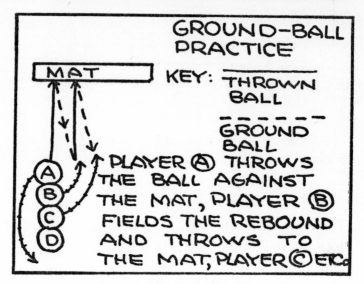

Drill No. 117

(c) To start the drill, the first player in line throws the ball against the mat.

(d) The next man waits until the ball bounces off the mat and then charges the ball, fields it, and throws it against the mat.

(e) Fielder goes to the end of the line and waits his turn.

(f) Speed of the practice may be increased by the intensity of the throws.

(g) Coach stresses all the fundamentals of fielding and throwing a ground ball.

118. Fielder who has lost confidence

The purpose of this drill is to develop the confidence of a player who has made several errors.

Procedure:

(a) Must teach correct fundamentals.

(b) Take player to the side so as not to interfere with regular practice.

(c) Hit hard grounders at him.

(d) No throw is necessary so he can give undivided attention to his fielding.

(e) Next make him take three or four steps, stop, and field the ball.

(f) Finally hit slow balls that he must come in at full speed to field.

(g) Half an hour of this should develop confidence.

119. Glove drill

The purpose of this drill is to teach the fundamentals of catching the ball with the glove. Many fielders have a rigid hand and glove resulting in many fumbles.

Procedure:

(a) Line up infielders in one line.

(b) In turn the coach rolls the ball to the infielder.

(c) Infielder catches the ball with his glove only.

(d) Free hand is held behind back.

(e) Upon catching the ball the fielder tosses it with the glove to the previous fielder, who rolls it to the coach.

(f) Coach finally hits the ball to the infielders who repeat procedure.

(g) This drill should be used out-of-doors as well.

(h) Coach stresses glove to the ground, out in front, wide base, follow ball into glove, give with ball and clutch ball.

Conclusion:

If a boy can play catch he can play baseball. Therefore, these simple fundamentals, well taught and practiced often, will enable anyone to play baseball adequately.

Chapter 10

Infield Defensive Drills

IN DEVELOPING A TEAM'S INNER DEFENSE, IT IS NECES-
sary to drill at times in pairs, in groups, or as a unit. The following are drills that will teach and provide practice in
the responsibilities of each individual of the infield. Players must learn the habits and become familiar with each
other's styles of fielding and throwing; this can only be
accomplished by working together continually.

PRE-SEASON INDOORS

120. Two-man fielding drill

The purpose of this drill is to improve hand-eye coordination of fielding a ground ball.

Procedure:

(a) Two players, "A" and "B", face each other six
feet apart.

Drill No. 120

(b) "A" uses a glove and is the fielder.

(c) "A" lobs the ball about shoulder high to "B".

(d) "B" pats the ball with the palm of his hand so that it bounces toward "A" who fields the ball and lobs it back to "B".

(e) Repeat procedure, only vary direction and bounce of ball, patting it so that "A" will have to scoop the ball to his left and right.

(f) When one player finishes four rounds change assignments.

(g) Many players can work in a small area.

121. Fielding ground balls by an infielder and making the play to first base

The purpose of this drill is to teach infielders how to field ground balls and throw to first base.

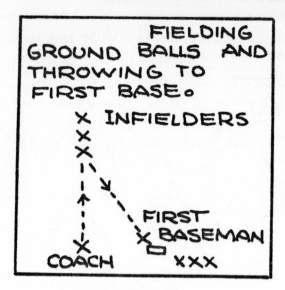

Drill No. 121

Procedure:

(a) Two units can be used at one time.

(b) Line first basemen up at bases which are about 30 feet from a line of infielders.

(c) Coach or pitcher hits ball slowly to infielders who field the ball and throw it to first base.

(d) First basemen line up properly, shift and stretch.

(e) Coach checks proper form in fielding, playing the bounce, and throwing.

(f) Coach, after checking one line, moves to the other.

(g) Coach modifies by hitting to the right and left.

(h) Line players up so they will have room to run about 15 feet to the right to field the ball and throw to first.

(i) Repeat and line up so they have room to run to the left.

(j) Hitters alternate so as to avoid collisions.

122. Second and short drill

The purpose of this drill is to develop the technique of executing the double play.

Procedure:

(a) Line up shortstops, second basemen and first basemen one behind the other in their respective positions.

(b) Coach stands approximately at the pitcher's box and throws ground balls to the shortstops, first directly at them, then to the third base side, and then to the second base side.

(c) In each case the shortstop must make the proper throw to the second baseman who foots the base for the forceout. The second baseman should know at least two methods of footing the base.

(d) Repeat procedure rolling the ball to the second baseman, directly at him, toward first base and then toward second. Execute correct throws and foot the base making the forceout. Should know at least two methods.

(e) After footing the base at second base has been mastered, the infielders throw to first.

(f) Throw into a net or canvas if area is not large enough.

(g) Drills start at slow speed and gradually speed up, but seldom go at full speed.

(h) Coach then varies the drill by mixing up the players he rolls the ball to.

(i) Coach stresses throws to second base, approach to second base, footwork, and throwing to first base.

(j) Coach finally hits the ball and procedure continues.

123. Basemen's putout drill

The purpose of this drill is to teach the technique of tagging a sliding runner.

Procedure:

(a) Primarily for third basemen, shortstops and second basemen.

(b) Use a baseman, a runner and a thrower.

(c) Tie two mats together, shellacked covers or made of rubber.

(d) Line up basemen at side of the base about six feet away.

(e) Put runner about 15 feet back.

(f) At signal from the thrower the runner breaks and slides into the base as the baseman covers the bag.

(g) Ball is thrown or lobbed underhand to the baseman who tags the runner.

(h) The coach stresses all the techniques of covering the bag and tagging the runner.

124. Bunt defense drill

The purpose of this drill is to teach the defense for the bunt.

Procedure:

(a) Use a complete infield, pitcher, catcher and a bunter.

(b) Place bases 90 feet apart or as near this distance as possible.

(c) Pitcher throws easily to the plate.

(d) Bunter bunts to *either* side and becomes a runner.

(e) As ball is pitched, the pitcher, first baseman and third baseman break toward home.

(f) Shortstop covers second and second baseman covers first.

(g) Catcher calls the play by designating who should field the ball and where ball should be thrown.

(h) Catcher goes to third base if third baseman fields the ball.

(i) If any other player fields the ball, the third baseman retreats and covers third.

(j) Other situations are then called out, such as, "Runners on first and second, no outs," "Bases filled, one out," and others.

(k) Runners are placed on bases, pitcher pitches and defensive players move into the correct defensive pattern and complete the play.

125. Double play drill

The purpose of this drill is to teach the player how to analyze the double play situation.

Procedure:

(a) Use catchers, first basemen, second basemen, shortstops and third basemen.

(b) Spare players line up at their respective positions.

(c) The coach hits to either side of second base.

(d) The player at the head of each line completes the double play and goes to the end of the line.

(e) As a modification, call a play situation such as, "Bases loaded, get two, home to first."

(f) Then hit a slow roller to be fielded on the run, thrown home and then to first.

(g) Players learn to analyze situations, varying their play according to speed of the hit, closeness to the base, the situation in regard to runners, etc.

126. Shortstop play on wide balls

The purpose of this drill is to teach the timid shortstop to go into the hole.

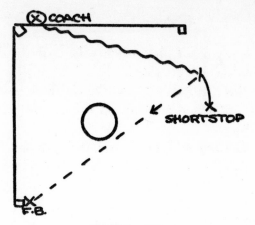

Drill No. 126

Procedure:

(a) Third baseman sits out.

(b) Coach hits the ball toward third.

(c) Shortstop must go in the hole to field the ball.

(d) He throws the ball to first.

(e) Coach finally mixes them up to develop nimbleness afoot, ability to field, pivot and throw.

(f) Coach stresses trying for every ball hit in the hole at third and over second.

127. Second baseman on wide balls

The purpose of this drill is to teach the second baseman to go into the hole.

Procedure:

(a) Place first baseman on the base.

(b) Coach hits ball toward first baseman.

(c) Second baseman fields the ball, pivots and throws to first base.

(d) Coach then hits ball over second.

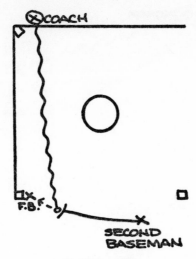

Drill No. 127

(e) Coach then mixes them up to develop nimble-ness afoot, ability to field, pivot and throw.

(f) Coach stresses trying for every ball wherever hit.

PRE-SEASON OUTDOORS

The outdoor practice of the infielders should include the drills on bunt defense, double plays, fielding all types of balls and throwing, to adjust to outdoor conditions. In these drills the coach should use runners whenever pos-sible.

128. Early season outdoors drill

This drill is used the first day or two so as to prevent sore arms and pulled muscles.

Procedure:

(a) Place all fielders at half distance.

(b) Hit grounders to each; they throw at ¼ speed.

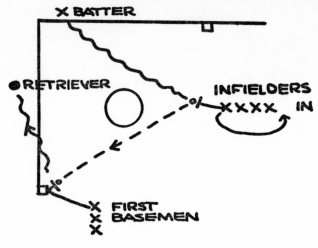

Drill No. 128

(c) Use two first basemen so each can move off the base after the play.

(d) Two balls may be used.

(e) Coach checks form and speed in getting ball away.

129. Early season variation

The purpose of this drill is to get in plenty of early practice on fielding ground balls.

Procedure:

(a) Use three fungo hitters with several baseballs apiece.

(b) One coach hits to third basemen.

(c) One coach hits to shortstops and second basemen behind second.

(d) Another coach hits to the first basemen.

(e) Fielder rolls ball back to a retriever at each spot.

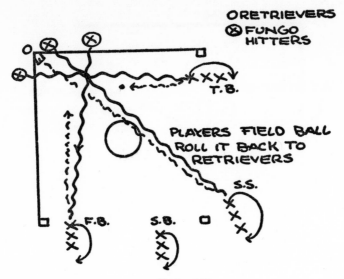

Drill No. 129

Variation:

(a) One coach hits to third baseman and shortstop in their positions.

(b) They throw to a player near the pitcher's mound.

(c) One coach hits to second baseman who throws to first.

130. For flinchers

The purpose is to develop a player's confidence in fielding a ground ball.

Procedure:

(a) Use several balls.

(b) Hit to one player only.

(c) He fields the ball and flips it to a retriever.

(d) He hustles back to position and prepares to field the ball again.

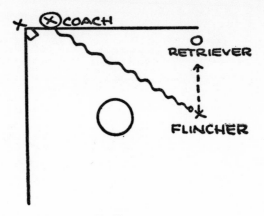

Drill No. 130

COMPETITIVE SEASON

The last fifteen minutes every day should involve a snappy infield practice. During this practice every fielding situation that comes up in a game should be repeated, including pop flies.

Chapter 11

Team Defensive Drills

FOLLOWING THE PERIOD OF DRILLING THE PLAYERS on the various fundamentals of infield play, it becomes necessary to mould these fundamentals into a team pattern. By this time each player or combination of players should know and be familiar with the responsibilities and duties concerned in playing his position. How well the fundamentals have been mastered will show up in team drills. The coach's job should now be more concerned with a general all around development of his team in working together as a unit.

131. Bunt defense drill

The purpose of this drill is to develop teamwork and practice the defense for the bunt.

Procedure:

(a) Use complete team.

(b) Second team act as bunters and runners.

(c) Pitcher works from a stretch and throws strikes.

(d) Infielders carry out their assignments.

(e) Outfielders back up the bases.

(f) Every bunt situation should be covered.

(g) Change pitchers and allow regulars to bunt while second string take their places in the field.

(h) Coach makes corrections and stresses the duty of the catcher to call out the play clearly and quickly.

132. All-purpose diamond drill

The purpose of this drill is to give the team practice on its defensive plays.

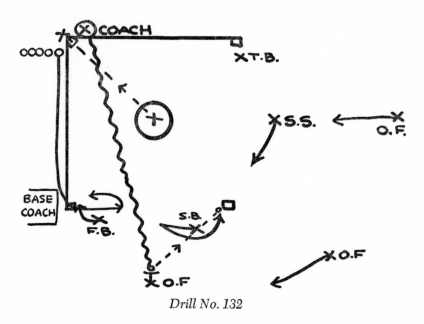

Drill No. 132

Procedure:

(a) Place first team in their regular playing positions.

(b) The second team and substitutes act as base runners.

(c) The pitcher pitches to the catcher to simulate a game.

(d) The coach, who is stationed in the batter's box, hits a ball out of his hand to any part of the field.

(e) A runner takes off for first from home plate.

(f) The ball is played as under game conditions.

(g) On each play the coach calls out number of outs, the inning and the score.

(h) The defense adjusts itself accordingly.

(i) After a runner has been thrown out he goes to the end of the line of runners at home plate and awaits his turn.

(j) Coach corrects all mistakes as they occur.

133. Team defensive drill

The purpose of this drill is to give the defensive team practice on making plays similar to those they will make during a game. At the same time pitchers and substitutes are getting their batting practice.

Procedure:

(a) Team takes their regular playing positions.

(b) Bases are unoccupied, but coach announces that imaginary runners are on a certain base, the number of outs, the inning and the score.

(c) Pitcher throws only strikes.

(d) Batter bunts first good pitch, swings at three pitches, and runs out the hit on the third swing as far as he can.

(e) Batter then returns to await his turn at bat.

(f) While waiting his turn at bat he can engage in bunting practice or swing a bat at imaginary balls.

(g) Coach corrects defensive mistakes as they occur.

134. Team defense on a single with runners on base

The purpose of this drill is to practice the defense for a one-base hit to the outfield.

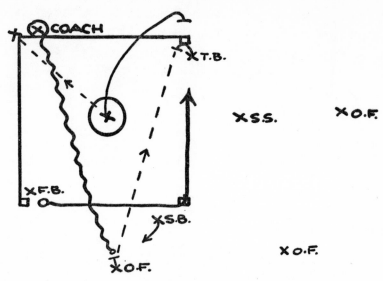

Drill No. 134 A

Procedure:

(a) Place regular team on the field in their positions.

(b) Use substitutes as runners.

(c) Pitcher pitches to the catcher from a stretch.

(d) Coach hits a ball from his hand through the infield.

(e) Place runner on first only and try to prevent him from reaching third on the hit (Drill 134 A).

(f) Place runner on second and try and prevent him from scoring on the hit (Drill 134 B).

(g) A runner takes off from home on the hit.

(h) Coach stresses cut-off techniques, pitcher backing up bases, and throwing to the proper bases.

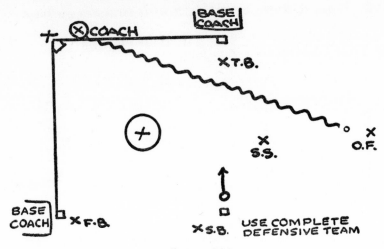

Drill No. 134 B

135. Extra-base-hit drill

The purpose of this drill is to practice the technique of handling the ball on a hit past the outfielder.

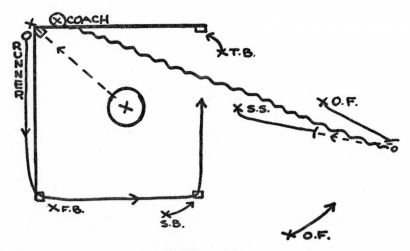

Drill No. 135 A

Procedure:

(a) Place regular team in their playing positions.
(b) Use substitutes as runners.
(c) Pitcher pitches to the catcher.
(d) Coach hits the ball from his hand past the out-fielders.

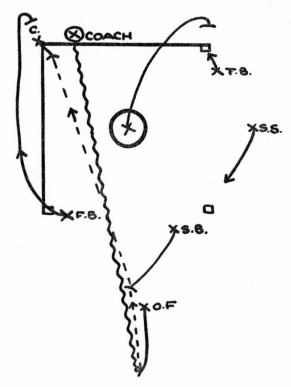

Drill No. 135 B

(e) Outfielders relay the ball to an infielder; the infielder to third base or to the catcher, depending on call by the infielder covering second base.
(f) Coach stresses types of throws, accurate throws,

target by infielder, pitcher backing up bases, and calling out the play by infielder at second base.

136. Throwing home after catching a fly ball with runner on third base

The purpose of this drill is to practice the technique of catching the ball and throwing home in attempt to catch the runner.

Procedure:

(a) Use regular outfielders in their positions.

(b) Use runner on third base.

(c) Runner tags up on the fly and attempts to score after the catch.

(d) Outfielder throws to the catcher at home plate trying to catch the runner.

(e) Coach stresses catching the ball by the outfielder, the crow hop step, the overhand throw, and the bounce throw to the catcher.

137. Pick-off and rundown drills

The purpose of this drill is to practice the pick-off plays and rundown procedures.

Procedure:

(a) Place regular team in their respective positions.

(b) Runners take turns getting picked off the base.

(c) Pitcher picks runner off first and races over to cover first if needed. Rundown follows between shortstop or second baseman and the first baseman.

(d) Pick-off play at second base; pitcher backs up third base. Rundown follows between shortstop or second baseman and third baseman.

(e) Pick-off play at third base; pitcher backs up

home. Rundown follows between third baseman or short-stop and the catcher.

(f) Coach stresses the various fundamentals of backing up bases and makes corrections as the need occurs.

138. Team defense using a batting "T"

The purpose of this drill is to practice all the defensive plays that may come up in a game.

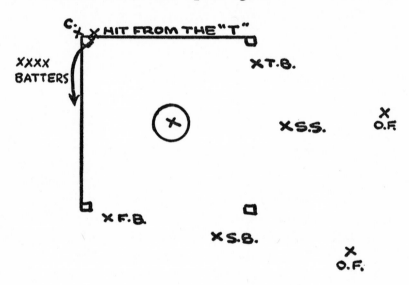

Drill No. 138

Procedure:

(a) Place all players in their respective positions including the pitcher.

(b) Place a batting "T" on home plate.

(c) Batter hits the ball off the "T" and becomes a baserunner.

(d) A regular game may be played.

(e) Allowing three outs, the runners return to the bench and await their turn at bat.

(f) Same team remains on the field indefinitely.

(g) By not using a pitcher to throw, many situations can be covered in a short period of time.

139. Pre-game infield and outfield practice

The purpose of this drill is to warm a team up and to prepare it for the defensive situations that will occur during the game. This drill effectively executed will also set the tempo of the game.

Procedure:

(a) Hit to the outfielders first.
    1. First round: hit the ball directly at the outfielder who throws to second base.
    2. Second round: hit the ball so that the outfielder must make a long throw to second.
    3. Third round: hit the ball so that the outfielder must run to the hole to field the ball and then throw it to third base.
    4. Fourth round: hit a fly ball that the outfielder can catch and make a normal throw to home.
    5. Fifth round: hit a grounder directly at the outfielder who charges the ball, fields it, and throws it home.

(b) Hitting to the infield.
    1. The ball should be hit so that the fielder can field it with ease and confidence. Coach does not try to get base hits.
    2. First round: Ball is hit on the ground di-

rectly at the infielder who throws it to the first baseman.

3. Second round: ball is hit so that the infielder must go to his left to make the short throw to first base.

4. Third round: ball is hit so that the infielder must go to his right and make the long throw to first.

5. Fourth round: ball is hit so that infielder must make a long throw to second base for a double play.

6. Fifth round: ball is hit so that infielder must make the short throw to second base for a double play.

7. Sixth round: Ball is hit slowly at the infielder so that he must charge the ball and make a hurried throw to first base.

8. Seventh round: a pop fly is hit to each infielder, who calls for the ball.

9. Eighth round: infielders in on the grass, ball is hit at them. Infielders field the ball and throw it home, catcher throws to first base.

10. When the ball is hit to the first baseman, he throws the ball to the shortstop, who throws it back to first.

11. At the end of each round the coach rolls the ball out in front of the plate and the catcher fields it and throws to the bases. First three rounds to first base, fourth and fifth rounds to second base, sixth round to third base.

12. After receiving the ball from the first baseman the catcher always throws it back to the base which the fielder who fielded the ball would normally cover. He in turn throws it

to the next base toward home, by way of third base.

13. Second basemen and shortstops practice their footwork on the double play rounds.
14. When catcher throws the ball back to the fielder at the base, the fielder should make a tag on an imaginary runner.
15. Practice should start out in a slow deliberate pace and gradually speed up to game tempo.

Chapter 12

Batting Drills

NATURAL ABILITY IS MORE ESSENTIAL IN HITTING THAN it is in any other phase of baseball; therefore, in selecting hitters this should be taken into consideration. Hitting's importance cannot, and should not, be underrated because it is felt that approximately 80 per cent of the team's offensive evolves around its hitting strength. Since each player has his own batting style, he should be encouraged to continue in it, unless the coach feels that the batter has developed some detrimental habits which will hinder his success as a hitter.

The following drills are designed to teach and aid in developing the fundamentals of hitting as well as to practice toward more efficiency in the skills already familiar to the hitter.

PRE-SEASON INDOORS

140. Bat control drill

This drill trains the arms and wrists to follow the movement of the ball.

BUNTING-BAT CONTROL

WORK PLAYERS IN GROUPS

Drill No. 140

Procedure:

(a) Work players in groups of six.

(b) Three players should face partners about five feet apart.

(c) Each should have a bat and use a grip similar to a bunting grip.

(d) Players attempt to keep the ball at a height of about six or seven feet as long as possible by bunting the ball across to each other.

(e) An underhand motion should be used.

(f) Coach stresses keeping the eye on the ball, and the action of the wrists and arms in bunting the ball.

141. Teaching the batting fundamentals

The purpose of this drill is to teach the fundamentals of batting.

Procedure:

(a) Provide each player with a bat.

(b) Coach explains and demonstrates the fundamentals.

(c) Players line up facing the coach allowing plenty of room to swing.

(d) On command the players swing at an imaginary pitched ball.

(e) The coach stresses stance, stride, swing, position of the head, grip and the follow through.

142. Follow-through drill

The purpose of this drill is to develop the follow through in swinging the bat. This drill will also aid in strengthening the wrists and arms.

Drill No. 142

Procedure:

(a) Place a medicine ball on a standard about waist high.

(b) Batter assumes a regular batting stance.

(c) Batter takes a normal swing and hits the medicine ball with the bat.

(d) First few attempts may not be too successful.

(e) Following several sessions at this type of swinging, the batter will be able to move the ball a considerable distance.

143. Breaking-the-wrist drill

The purpose of this drill is to teach the batter to break his wrists in swinging a bat.

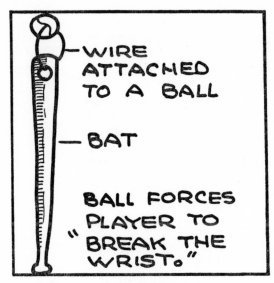

Drill No. 143

Procedure:

(a) A ball is attached to the end of a bat by a heavy wire.

(b) The ball is placed behind the bat.

(c) The batter assumes a normal batting stance and swings the bat as if hitting a ball.

(d) On the swing, the ball moves over the end of the bat and forces the bat to continue vigorously in its normal path.

(e) Coach stresses firm grip on the bat and proper follow through.

144. Swinging drill using a calibrated bat

The purpose of this drill is to teach and demonstrate the fundamentals necessary to get more velocity into a swing.

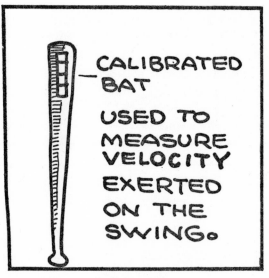

Drill No. 144

Procedure:

(a) Use a calibrated bat.

(b) Batter assumes his batting stance and swings the bat.

(c) The bat measures the amount of velocity exerted on the swing.

(d) If wrists are rotated correctly and at the time of impact with an imaginary ball, the velocity will increase.

(e) Continued swinging with this bat will develop a definite feeling of exerting force at the time of the wrist rotation.

145. Striding drill

The purpose of this drill is to develop the correct batting stride.

Procedure:

(a) Use a pitcher and a catcher.

(b) Batter assumes a normal batting stance with a bat.

(c) Pitcher throws to the catcher.

(d) Batter does not swing at the ball but merely takes his stride on each pitch.

(e) Batter should practice stepping in the right direction on each pitch and watching the ball all the way into the glove.

146. Swinging practice

The purpose of this drill is to develop a good swing.

Procedure:

(a) Batter holds bat correctly.

(b) Batter assumes his normal batting stance.

(c) Batter swings at an imaginary ball hitting it about two feet out in front of the body.

(d) To get a good follow through, batter should try and drive his bat through the ball.

(e) Vary the spot at which batters swing to get the idea of leveling off on pitches of different heights.

(f) Batter keeps his eye on the spot as though he were watching the ball meet the bat.

(g) He times the swing so that his weight comes against the front leg as the bat meets an imaginary ball.

(h) Batter should practice this swing about fifty times a day, but should not take more than ten or fifteen swings at a time.

(i) Batters should keep bat around the house and practice at odd moments.

(j) When on the field and not otherwise occupied batters should pick up a bat and practice their swing.

(k) The swing must be done without thinking about it; therefore it should be practiced at any spare moment.

147. Hip-swing drill

The purpose of this drill is to teach the proper hip rotation used when swinging at a ball.

Procedure:

(a) Players face coach with their feet spread as in a normal stance.

(b) Hands are placed on hips.

(c) On command, players rotate their hips and take a short step in the direction of the rotation.

(d) Coach stresses a strong hip rotation and short step or stride.

148. Hip swing with dumbbells for hitting

The purpose of this drill is to develop a fast, strong hip whip essential in powerful hitting. Regular use of this swing with weight will help strengthen the muscles that produce the whip.

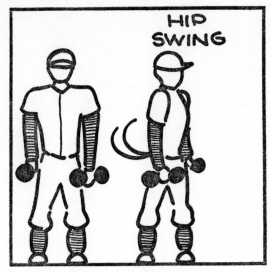

Drill No. 148

Procedure:

(a) Batters stand erect with feet comfortably spread (normal batting stance).

(b) Hold dumbbells in each hand (fairly heavy) at side, belt high.

(c) Twist to one side, moving both dumbbells.

(d) Reverse action and swing back.

(e) Use hip and side muscles only.

(f) Repeat 10 times to each side.

149. Batting "T" drill

The purpose of this drill is to teach and correct batting techniques.

Procedure:

(a) Perform at one end of the gym, against bleachers, basketball backboards, or in a small room.

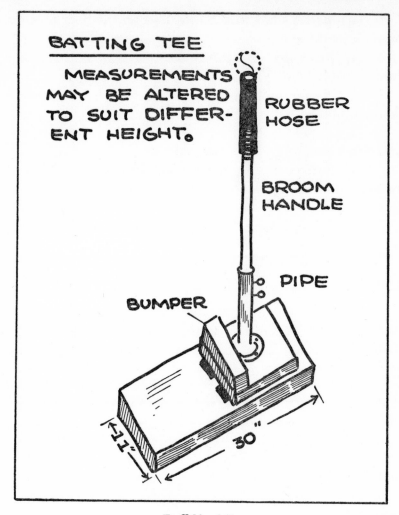

Drill No. 149

(b) Hang a net, canvas or mat in a position so that the ball will not bounce or deflect when hit.

(c) Place batting "T" about five feet from the net, canvas or mat.

(d) Batter takes his normal stance in a batter's box. (A batter's box is advisable.)

(e) Batter's box may be painted on the floor or put on with masking tape.

(f) Place the "T" so that the ball is located on the front edge of home plate.

(g) Batter does everything in batting that he would do on a pitched ball.

(h) Daily work at the "T" will condition the players and eliminate early season soreness.

(i) Batters should take at last fifty to seventy-five swings a day; any more will prove tiring and therefore useless.

(j) Coach corrects and instructs each individual as he takes his turn at the batting "T".

150. Directions to build a batting "T"

The batting "T" is a very inexpensive piece of equipment that can be constructed by the manual training or maintenance department of the school, or by anyone handy with tools. There are several types on the market, but a good sturdy one that is simple to make is the most practical. The following are the directions by which a batting "T" may be constructed.

(a) Baseboard: 30 inches long by 11 inches wide and 1%16 inches thick.

(b) Topboard: 12 inches long by 2 inches wide and ⅞ inch thick.

(c) Attach an extra piece of wood, 2 x 2 x 9 inches, to act as a reinforcement and a bumper on the front edge of the top board.

(d) Two six-inch strap hinges should be bolted on.

(e) Use two metal mending plates which are screwed on to make top board level. These plates also act as bumpers.

(f) Use nine-inch piece of one-inch pipe with two thumb screws.

(g) Thread pipe at one end.

(h) The threaded end screws into a one-inch flange which is bolted through the top board.

(i) Place the flange as near the front of the top board as possible.

(j) Broom handles are used as sticks and should vary in length: 12, 22, 34 and 44 inches long.

(k) Friction tape will be needed to build up the end of the broom handle which is generally ⅞ inch thick.

(l) Use radiator hose one inch in diameter and one foot long.

(m) Place the radiator hose on the stick about three inches.

(n) The various length of sticks will allow for different heights of balls.

(o) These measurements and directions may be altered to suit taste and materials on hand.

151. "Look them over or call them"

The purpose of this drill is to develop the ability of the batter in determining whether a pitch is a ball or strike.

Procedure:

(a) Batter stands in the batter's box in regular batting stance.

(b) Participants are a catcher, pitcher, umpire and scorer.

(c) Each batter gets ten pitched balls (or some other set number).

(d) If batter considers the pitch a strike, he drops his bat and watches the ball go into the catcher's glove.

(e) If he considers the pitch a ball he withdraws his bat.

(f) The umpire calls each pitch.

(g) The scorer credits the batter with each correct call and keeps a score on all participants.

152. "Look them over" practice (variation)

This drill is used to develop the batter's conception of the strike zone.

Procedure:

(a) Batter stands in a batter's position while the pitcher is pitching to the catcher at the pitching strings.

(b) Batter watches the ball into the catcher's glove.

(c) Batter must concentrate and develop a definite impression of his strike zone.

153. Pepper game

The purpose of this drill is to develop the hand and eye coordination used in making the bat meet the ball. This drill also acts as an aid in practicing the fundamentals of fielding by the various fielders.

Procedure:

(a) Several players face the batter about 15 feet away.

(b) Batter hits the ball to each player in turn.

(c) Batter watches the ball hit the bat and completes a follow through.

(d) Batter doesn't apply a great deal of force in his swing but merely goes through the motions of meeting the ball.

(e) For interest and motivation, number players;

every time a fielder misses the ball he goes to the end of the line.

(f) If batter misses he goes to the end of the line and the head man becomes the hitter.

(g) Coach should stress watching the ball and controlling the direction of his hit.

PRE-SEASON OUTDOORS

Upon moving outdoors the batting and bunting practices assume full scale in every way. The fundamentals having been practiced inside, they now must be practiced under conditions as game-like as possible. Most batting will now take place in a variety of team batting practice drills. Any work on fundamentals will now be centered on the player who has glaring weaknesses. A batting "T", however, should be available for use at all times to help correct faults.

154. Early season batting practice

The purpose of this drill is to aid players to follow the ball throughout its flight.

Procedure:

(a) Pitcher and catcher throw.

(b) Batter takes his position at the plate and watches the ball.

(c) With his bat on shoulder, he watches the ball all the way to the plate, following it with his eyes.

(d) He should not lose sight of the ball due to any movement of the head or body.

(e) If he pulls away (timid) he should face the pitcher squarely.

(f) As player gains confidence he gradually turns back to the normal position.

(g) Catcher or umpire should call balls and strikes.

155. Batting stride drills

The purpose of these drills is to suggest methods which may be used to correct faulty strides.

(a) Stepping away from the ball
  1. Draw a line in the batter's box from the toe of the rear foot to the front of the box where batter's foot should land.
  2. Coach checks after each swing to be sure that batter's foot is up to the line.
(b) Overstrider
  1. Construct a box or a frame 40 to 44 inches long, 16 inches wide and 6 inches high.
  2. Place batter in the batter's box where he ordinarily takes his position to bat.
  3. Player must remain in this box while batting.
(c) Overstrider
  1. Place mud in the front section of the batter's box.
  2. Batter will lose footing if he steps in the mud.

156. Developing the poor hitter

The purpose of this drill is to aid in teaching the very poor hitter how to improve his hitting.

Procedure:

(a) Use a pitcher who has good control (coach may have to pitch).

(b) Pitcher throws slowly at first, gradually increasing the speed.

(c) Batter assumes a stance just wider than his hips.

(d) Batter should look at a few pitches before starting his swings.

(e) Batter is not allowed to stride when he swings.

(f) Gradually allow batter to take a short step on his swing.

(g) Meeting the ball squarely should improve greatly.

157. Striding faults drill

The purpose of this drill is to aid in the correction of faulty strides.

Procedure:

(a) Use a pitcher with good control.

(b) Place a bat in the batter's box so that a batter will step on it when he strides.

(c) For the overstrider, place the bat in front of the box where the striding foot normally lands.

(d) For a "bucket stepper," place the bat to the side so that the batter will be conscious of it.

(e) For the batter who steps back, place the bat against his rear foot.

158. Place hitting

The purpose of this drill is to practice place hitting.

Procedure:

(a) Use one round of batting practice.

(b) Batter announces to the coach privately to which field he intends to hit the ball.

(c) His success will tell a coach of his educability in the art of place hitting.

159. Batting drill to gain confidence

The purpose of this drill is to build a player's confidence in his ability to follow a pitched ball.

Procedure:

(a) Place all fielders in right field.

(b) Right-hand hitter must hit to right field.

(c) If batter hits to the left of second base, he must retrieve the ball himself.

(d) After a couple of long trips, the batter will watch the ball more closely.

(e) Reverse should be done for left-handers.

160. Mirror drill

This drill is a method by which a player may check his form in batting and bunting.

Procedure:

(a) Use a mirror approximately 60 inches long that can be raised or lowered.

(b) Mirror should be mounted on rollers so that it can be moved from place to place.

(c) Batter should observe his swing for faults.

161. Team batting practice drills

The purpose of these drills is to present a variety of team batting practices which cover many play situations, and which also may be motivating. These drills must be closely supervised by the coach.

162. Variation 1: a fast moving batting practice

(a) Use regular batting order.

(b) Allow only three men at cage at a time.

(c) In order each batter takes three hits and a bunt.

(d) Following his turn the batter returns to his fielding position.

(e) Pitcher pitches for about 15 minutes.

(f) Catchers each spell each other.

163. Variation 2: practice against various pitchers

(a) Use regular batting order.

(b) Batters take about fifteen swings.

(c) Half of pitches are curve balls.

(d) Curves should be thrown on request.

164. Variation 3: to keep batting practice moving

(a) Keep squad small, not exceeding six, allowing players to bat more often.

(b) Allow each man to take several turns at bat.

(c) Then let this squad go to the field while another squad comes to bat.

(d) It may be possible to change squads a number of times during a practice session.

(e) Each batter should hit three and bunt one.

165. Variation 4: situation hitting

(a) Place a defensive team on the field.

(b) Place a runner on first with no outs.

(c) One round of all plays is possible with this situation.

(d) Repeat same procedure with runners on second, third and then with bases full.

(e) Control count on the batter to speed up practice.

(f) Use base coaches.

166. Variation 5: control count

(a) Use runners and defensive team.

(b) Give batter one strike to move the runners.

(c) Batter runs out the hit.

167. Variation 6: one swing drill

(a) Use five or six batters.

(b) Permit one swing.

(c) Batter must hit ball safely.

(d) If he misses, hits a foul, or doesn't run out hit, batter goes to the field and fielder comes in.

(e) Pitcher uses ¾ speed fast ball.

(f) Increase speed as practice continues.

168. Variation 7: two balls and one strike count

(a) Any number of players can be used.

(b) Each batter goes to bat with a two-and-one count on him.

(c) When player strikes out or scores a run, he takes a place in the field.

(d) Hitters become more conscious of hitting the ball, and more aggressive at the plate. They must be ready to hit the first good pitch and then learn to bear down if the next pitch is a strike. They also learn that they cannot afford to be fooled.

(e) Players get to bat more often.

(f) This drill has many excellent features and possible adaptations.

169. Variation 8:

(a) Use batting order.

(b) Determine the number of swings the batter may take.

(c) Then allow one more.

(d) If batter gets a solid hit on a grounder or a line drive through the infield, he continues batting until he misses.

170. Variation 9:

(a) Allow outfielders to hit first; they then shag flys.

(b) Then all infielders hit; they have been fielding grounders while outfielders batted.

(c) After hitting, each player should move to an area where bunting practice can be conducted. Practice sacrifice as well as drag bunts.

171. Variation 10: all-purpose batting drill

(a) Use one round every day, including pre-game batting practice.

(b) Each batter is allowed six swings.

(c) First pitch is a hit and run.

(d) Second pitch is a squeeze bunt.

(e) On the next three pitches, the batter hits away.

(f) On the sixth pitch, the batter drag bunts, and runs the bunt out. Batter should sacrifice bunt if not adept at drag bunting.

(g) Bunter now becomes a runner at first, runs to third on hit and run and scores on squeeze.

(h) Drill continues until all batters desired have gone through the procedure.

(i) Batters get practice in all the offensive situations that will come up in a game, including running the bases.

172. Variation 11: small squad batting practice

The purpose of this drill is to keep a small squad active and give more enjoyment to the practice.

Procedure:

(a) Divide group into squads of four.

(b) Group one bats first, then two, then three.

(c) Each group has its own catcher.

(d) Pitcher works normal batting practice stint.

(e) After three outs, next group moves in to bat.

(f) As a variation, each team could bat for twenty minutes.

(g) Other variations may be used to fit the situation.

COMPETITIVE SEASON

Several of the preceding drills should be used from time to time during regular practice sessions as a motivation factor as well as to break the monotony of doing the same thing every day. In addition to this, from time to time you may find occasion to use the following.

173. Tuneup for a fast-ball pitcher

The purpose of this drill is to prepare the team to face a very fast pitcher.

Procedure:

(a) Use at least for two days before the game.

(b) Pitchers work from 50 feet away instead of 60.

(c) Batters may not hit ball at first but will adjust as practice continues and begin to hit for base hits more often.

(d) When you move pitcher back to normal distance he will have more trouble throwing a fast ball by the batters.

(e) Repeat procedure for a notorious curve ball or slow ball pitcher.

Conclusion:

Scoring runs and hitting are the most thrilling aspects in baseball; this reason alone is enough to encourage long practice and achievement. However, this being so, adequate work on the other phases of baseball, without which base hits would be of little value, should not be neglected.

Chapter 13

Bunting Drills

ONE OF THE FUNDAMENTALS OF BASEBALL THAT DOES
not get its share of attention and practice is the art of bunting. Most youngsters and professional players as well are
very inept when it comes to bunting the ball under the
pressure of a game situation. Yet, when asked if they know
how to bunt, the answer is usually an enthusiastic yes. If
it weren't for the coach who insists that a player bunt, once
or twice, during a batting practice, no one would ever get
any practice at bunting. The few times that a coach has a
concentrated bunting practice are not enough to master
this very important phase of baseball. It is something that
has to be worked at seriously and continuously.

A college or a high school team has a place for a
good bunter, especially if he has a little speed. The good
hitter who can also bunt has a great advantage in that his
threat of bunting keeps the defensive players on edge and
they can't play as deep for him as they ordinarily would.

It is imperative that a player know how to bunt if he is to be of greatest possible value to his team. A good hitter should be a good bunter and weak hitters must be good bunters. The following drills, if worked at conscientiously, will be of great help in the development of a dependable bunter.

PRE-SEASON INDOORS

174. Bunting fundamentals drill

The purpose of this drill is to teach the fundamentals of bunting.

Procedure:

(a) Provide each player with a bat.

(b) Coach demonstrates and explains the fundamentals he desires.

(c) Players spread out facing the coach and, on command, assume a bunting stance.

(d) Coach corrects those with poor form.

(e) Procedure is repeated several times.

(f) Finally the bunters assume their normal batting stance.

(g) On command, or as the coach goes through the motion of pitching from a stretch, they pivot and take a bunting stance.

(h) Coach makes corrections and repeats the procedure until technique is mastered.

(i) Finally the bunters practice the drag or push bunt.

(j) Batters won't master this technique of the drag bunt at this time but will become familiar with the technique for later practice sessions.

175. Bunting fundamentals practice drill

The purpose of this drill is to practice the fundamentals of bunting.

Procedure:

(a) Organize players in groups of threes; three such groups can work in a 50-foot gymnasium floor.

(b) One player pitches, one fields the bunted ball and the third bunts the ball.

(c) Bunter is allowed five bunts at a turn.

(d) After each turn, the three men rotate.

(e) Pitcher throws about ½ speed as near 60 feet away from the bunter as possible.

(f) Batter should assume bunting stance on the first round to get the feeling of catching the ball with the bat.

(g) On second round, and thereafter, batter assumes a batting position and pivots to the bunting stance when the pitcher releases the ball.

(h) Coach watches closely and makes corrections, warning also about carelessness in executing the bunt.

176. Bunting placement drill

The purpose of this drill is to practice placing the bunt.

Procedure:

(a) Use a catcher and pitcher who throws at half speed.

(b) Batter is allowed four bunts.

(c) One bunt is placed down first baseline, one down third baseline; a squeeze bunt and finally a drag or push bunt are also used.

(d) Coach checks form and makes corrections.

177. Drag bunt drill

Drag bunting, being somewhat different from regular bunting in execution, needs additional practice and individual attention.

Procedure:

(a) Use a pitcher and catcher.

(b) Pitcher throws at ¾ speed.

(c) Batter attempts to drag or push the ball past the pitcher towards first or third.

(d) Coach watches each batter closely to see if he is giving away his intentions, and to correct any unnecessary movements.

178. "Look them over or call them"

The purpose of this drill is to develop the ability of the batter to determine whether a pitch is a ball or a strike. Bunter bunts only strikes.

Procedure:

(a) Use a pitcher, catcher and an umpire.

(b) Batter assumes his batting position and pivots to a bunting position when pitcher releases the ball.

(c) Batter does not bunt the ball.

(d) If the ball is a strike, he drops his bat, and, if it is a ball, he brings his bat back.

(e) The umpire calls each pitch.

(f) The scorer credits the batter for each correct call and keeps the scores of all participants.

(g) Coach stresses bunting only strikes, and checks on bunting form.

179. Pepper game

The purpose of this drill is to practice the fundamentals of bunting. It also trains the fielders as well.

Procedure:

(a) Batter assumes bunting stance and bunts the ball to the fielders.

(b) Batter assumes bunting stance and bunts the ball to the fielders.

(c) Bunter loses his turn when he misses the ball, providing it was a good throw.

(d) Fielder at the head of the line moves into the bunt position.

(e) If fielder misses the ball, he goes to the end of the line.

(f) Batter must bunt the ball, not half-swing at it.

(g) Pepper games are conducive to horseplay if not properly supervised.

PRE-SEASON OUTDOORS

Most of the bunting will now be practiced in conjunction with team defensive work. It will also get a little attention in the daily batting practice sessions. When batting practice is going on there is no reason why a separate area cannot be used for bunting practice, using a pitcher and catcher.

180. Timid bunter

This drill is designed to teach the bunter to hold his position in the batter's box when bunting.

Procedure:

(a) The bunting position is an unnatural position for many batters.

(b) Bunter faces the pitcher in good form and watches the ball all the way to the plate.

(c) He doesn't attempt to bunt the ball.

(d) Watching the ball in this manner may be necessary for several pitches.

(e) Then allow the batter to bunt the ball.

(f) Finally the batter is allowed to resume a normal batter's stance, then pivot into a bunting position before bunting the ball.

(g) If batter still is shy, drill should be repeated until he has mastered his fear.

181. Bunt control drill

This drill is used to practice control of the bunted ball.

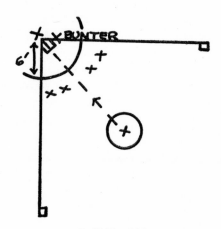

Drill No. 181

Procedure:

(a) Draw a semi-circle with a six-foot diameter in front of the plate.

(b) Bunters attempt to bunt the ball so it will hit inside this circle.

(c) Ball will roll the desired distance most of the time.

COMPETITIVE SEASON

Daily practice is required in bunting more than in many other phases of baseball, because the tendency is to become careless about it. It is often necessary for a coach to spend a whole session several times during the season on bunting alone. There is no reason for players' failure to bunt when called upon to do so. These failures do occur because he has not been conscientious in his practice and in developing the right attitudes toward this all-important fundamental.

182. Bunting with confidence

The purpose of this drill is to prepare a team to face a fast-ball pitcher.

Procedure:

(a) Pitcher pitches from 50 feet out.
(b) Batter bunts five pitches.
(c) Coach corrects faults that anyone might have.
(d) If a boy can skillfully bunt at this distance, he will have more confidence at 60 feet.

Conclusion:

A good bunting team will win many close ball games and break other games wide open. This can only be done by the mastery of, and continued practice in, the fundamentals of bunting.

Chapter 14

Baserunning Drills

THE IMPORTANCE OF PRACTICE IN THE FUNDAMENTALS of baserunning cannot be overemphasized. Good baserunning depends on a quick start and getaway. One requisite of a baseball player is that he have good running speed. Very often the fastest runner is not the best baserunner, generally because of faulty starts. The following drills are methods of practicing proper starts and running techniques. Each drill is a basic part of the team's offense and fits naturally into the method of play.

183. Starting and running practice

The purpose of this drill is to teach the proper method of starting and then running.

Procedure:

(a) While indoors use end lines of gym. Outdoors use the lanes of the running track or the foul lines of the baseball field as the starting lines, and run toward center field.

(b) Line up approximately six players at a time.

(c) Each assumes a stance similar to one used on taking a lead off base.

(d) On command the six players break and run at full speed for about 30 yards, slow down gradually, and then return to the end of their line. Adjust distances for indoor practice.

(e) Next group steps up to position and repeats procedure.

(f) Coach positions himself so that he can observe each runner closely and make corrections.

184. Starting at home plate

The purpose of this drill is to teach the proper method of starting from home after hitting a ball.

Procedure:

(a) Players line up at home and, in turn, step into the batter's box.

(b) Player should swing a bat at an imaginary ball and start for first base.

(c) Coach observes closely the footwork in starting and makes corrections.

185. Running to first base

The purpose of this drill is to teach proper running form.

Procedure:

(a) Line up players at home plate.

(b) Each swings at an imaginary ball and takes off for first base.

(c) Running at full speed, the player steps on the base, continues on past it and slows down gradually.

(d) Coach stresses start, pumping the arms, body lean, stride, eyes straight ahead, listening to the coach, stepping on the base, and slowing down.

(e) Coach should use a stopwatch on the runners.

186. Rounding first base

This drill is to practice starts, running form, and rounding first base.

Procedure:

(a) Line up players at home to take their turn swinging a bat and running to second base.

(b) Stop watch should be used on each player.

(c) Coach observes and corrects method of rounding the base, as well as all baserunning fundamentals.

(d) Finally, run all the way to home plate rounding bases properly.

187. Determining leads off first base

The purpose of this drill is to teach a player how to arrive at an adequate lead off first base.

Procedure:

(a) Use a pitcher, catcher, and first baseman.

(b) Line up approximately six players at a time along the foul line, the first in line being at the base.

(c) The pitcher takes a stretch and the runners move off the base and assume a ready position.

(d) Pitcher throws several times to first base and on each occasion the runner returns to the foul line.

(e) After each throw to first base the runner adjusts

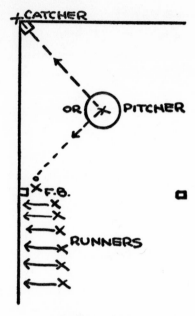

Drill No. 187

his next lead so that he can finally determine what his normal lead should be.

(f) When the pitcher throws to the catcher the runners all break for second.

(g) Next set of runners now move into position at the foul line.

(h) Practice continues until the fundamentals are well understood by each runner.

188. Returning to first base

The purpose of this drill is to teach the method of starting to second base and returning to first base.

Procedure:

(a) Use the preceding procedure with a batter in position.

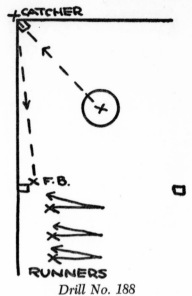

Drill No. 188

(b) Runners break for second on the pitch.

(c) When the ball passes the batter, the runner returns to first base.

(d) Catcher throws to the first baseman.

(e) Coach stresses leaving the base, stance, break, and return to the base.

189. Drill for lead at second base and return to the base

This drill teaches the proper lead at second.

Procedure:

(a) This may be practiced in the same method as at first, use shortstop and second baseman.

(b) It is practical to use one runner at a time.

(c) Pitcher should throw several pitches to second base so runner may adjust his distance.

(d) When pitcher throws home, the runner breaks for third.

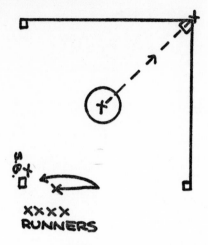

Drill No. 189

(e) Runner returns to second base when catcher receives the ball.

(f) Coach stresses distance of lead, stance, break toward third, and return to second base.

190. Lead off third

The purpose of this drill is to teach the lead off third.

Procedure:

(a) Runners take turns taking leads.

(b) Pitcher throws to home and runner studies his moves.

(c) Runner assumes a lead, moves toward home on the pitch and returns to the third base correctly.

(d) Runner then practices a lead and a break for a steal of home.

(e) Coach stresses the fundamentals and makes any corrections necessary.

191. Sliding

Sliding practice fundamentals can be practiced inside. The purpose of this drill is to teach the fundamentals of sliding.

Procedure:

(a) Equipment necessary are two sets of gym mats, sweat pants, baseball pants and sliding pads.

(b) Remove sneakers and work in stocking feet.

(c) Players line up at the mats.

(d) In turn and from a stationary position take off as one would in sliding.

(e) It will take several attempts before player gets the feel of the sliding technique.

(f) Continue drill from a short run.

(g) Coach stresses take off, hands, landing, height, and hooking the base.

PRE-SEASON OUTDOORS

All the pre-season indoor drills should now be practiced outdoors to adjust to outdoor conditions and as near game conditions as possible. While these drills are specifically for the runners, they can also be used to give extra work to the pitchers and fielders in their pick-off and rundown fundamentals.

192. Running to second base

The purpose of this drill is to teach the runner the correct procedure to follow in determining whether to continue on to second on a base hit.

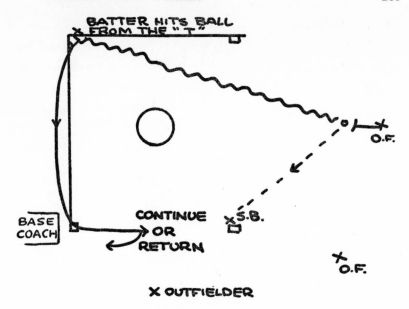

Drill No. 192

Procedure:

(a) Use only outfielders and an infielder stationed at second base.

(b) Place a batting "T" at home plate and allow the batter to hit from the "T".

(c) Place base coach in coach's box.

(d) Each batter in turn hits and takes off for first, rounds the base and heads for second.

(e) Coach stresses baserunning fundamentals and the outfielder gets practice in fielding and throwing.

193. Runners advance drill

The purpose of this drill is to teach the runners when to advance on batted balls.

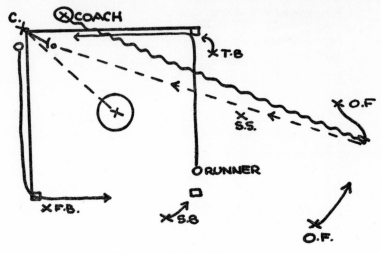

Drill No. 193

Procedure:

(a) Use a complete defensive team.

(b) Place runner at second base, with nobody out.

(c) Pitcher throws to the catcher.

(d) Coach hits the ball out of his hand on the ground.

(e) Runner advances according to where the ball is hit.

(f) Fielders play the ball and throw to proper base.

(g) Repeat procedure with one out.

(h) Place runners on third and repeat situations.

(i) Use coach at third to give instructions to runners.

194. All-purpose team drill

The purpose of this drill is to develop the technique of running and advancing on the bases. It also gives practice to the defense in all their defensive situations.

Procedure:

(a) Use a complete defensive team.

(b) Pitcher throws to the catcher.

(c) Coach hits the ball from his hand to any section of the field.

(d) Coaches are placed at first and third.

(e) When coach hits ball, a runner takes off for first and advances as far as he can.

(f) Runner remains on base and advances on next hit by the coach.

(g) Players get practice running the bases and receiving instructions from the base coach.

195. Outdoor sliding practice

The purpose of this drill is to practice the fundamentals of sliding.

Procedure:

(a) Use sliding pits, high jump pits, or soft grassy area, especially on rainy days.

(b) Review previous indoor drill starting from a stationary position.

(c) Players wear full gear, sliding pads, sneakers. Use spikes only after skill has been mastered.

(d) Place a base in appropriate position.

(e) Position a player at the base who takes an imaginary throw from one side of the base or the other.

(f) Runner uses a lead start, runs directly toward the base, takes off, slides and hooks the base properly.

(g) The side of the body the runner slides on depends on the side of the base that the fielder at the base receives the throw.

(h) Coach stresses distance and height of the take-off, position of the hands, position of the body on landing, side of the base to which the slide is made, and hooking the base.

COMPETITIVE SEASON

During this part of the season it is important to practice at least once a week, a drill that involves baserunning with base coaches and using team signals. These drills will also bring in other offensive techniques as well as many defensive maneuvers.

Conclusion:

The coach who practices his fundamentals and then continues periodic reviews is more likely to be a perennial winner. Poise and confidence on the bases can only be accomplished through concentrated practice sessions, and then applied in game conditions.

APPENDIX

I

Screening Candidates

IT IS NECESSARY WHEN FACED WITH LARGE SQUADS TO
eliminate quickly those who do not have the necessary
qualities you look for in selecting personnel. At the same
time it is important that each prospective player is con-
vinced that he has been given a fair chance at showing
what he can do. You are on sound ground if you have performance records to back up your decisions on the abili-
ties of those players who have to be cut.

The following are two procedures that can be used
as a basis for a team tryout:

196. Procedure for tryouts

(a) 50-yard dash using a stop watch.

(b) Baseball throw for distance, 10 tries from a line
250 feet from home plate.

(c) Baseball throw for accuracy, 10 tries using a six-
foot archery target.

(d) Batting for form and execution, 10 tries.

(e) Fielding for form and execution, 10 tries (five
on the ground, five in the air).

(f) The coach or an assistant should pitch and hit the ball for fielding.

(g) Allow 10 points for each activity.

197. Procedure for screening candidates

(a) 50-yard dash using a stop watch.

(b) Throw for distance by outfielders, 3 tries from a line 250 feet from home plate. Check on accuracy of direction and form.

(c) Infielders field and throw first from position of their choice. Check agility, coordination, good hands, and sureness of fielding.

(d) Infielders field and throw from the hole at shortstop to check on strength of their arms.

(e) All catchers in full gear throw from same spot in catcher's box.

(f) All things being equal in pitchers, select those with big hands over small.

(g) Hitting is checked last—allow ten swings with pitcher throwing ¾ speed.

II

Indoor Practice

THE FOLLOWING TWO-WEEK SCHEDULE OF INDOOR
drills is arranged to aid the coach in preparing and conditioning his team for the outdoor season. Much can be done indoors by careful planning of time and space. Care must be taken so that the element of danger is negligible. This program is based on a two hour daily practice session; and normally begins soon after the basketball season is over. In some areas more than two weeks may be available, if so the coach should alter his program to suit his needs.

First day—Monday

4:00   Coach explains to his team practice plans and organizes players into pairs according to position.

4:15   Reaction drill, No. 7.

4:25   Two man fielding drill, No. 120.

4:35   Fielding ground ball, No. 116.
       Catching fundamentals, Nos. 45, 48, 46, 47, 51.

4:45   Ground ball practice (variation) mats on wall, No. 117.

191

Catchers on fundamentals, Nos. 45, 48, 51, 46, 47.

4:55   Infielders play pepper, No. 153.
Outfielders use batting "T", No. 149.
Pitchers throw easy to catcher for form from a pumping position, Nos. 13, 14.

5:15   Outfielders at pepper.
Infielders to batting "T", No. 149.
Pitchers work on stretch and holding men on base, Nos. 13, 14 variation.

5:30   Pitchers at pepper.
Catchers at batting "T", No. 149.
Infielders field ground ball and throw to 1st baseman, No. 121.
Outfielders field ground balls and fly balls, Nos. 97, 98, 99.

5:45   Team conditioning drill, No. 3.

Second day—Tuesday

4:00   Drill No. 7
4:10   Drill No. 120.
4:20   Drill No. 116.
Catching drills, Nos. 45, 48, 46, 47, 51.
4:30   Drill No. 117.
Repeat catchers' drills.
4:45   Infielders at pepper.
Outfielders at "T".
Pitchers throwing to catchers for form from pump, Nos. 13, 14, 16.
5:00   Outfielders at pepper.
Infielders at batting "T".
Pitchers throwing to catchers for form from stretch, Nos. 13, 14, 16.

5:15 Pitchers at pepper.
Catchers at batting "T".
Outfielders fielding grounders and fly balls
and throwing.
Infielders in a line fielding and throwing to
first baseman.
5:30 Bunting practice, No. 175.
5:45 Team conditioning drill.

Third day—Wednesday

4:00 Drill No. 7
4:05 Drill No. 120.
4:10 Drill No. 116.
Catching fundamentals.
4:15 Drill No. 117.
Catching fundamentals.
4:20 Infielders at pepper.
Outfielders at "T".
Pitchers and catchers throwing for form from
pump, Nos. 13, 14, 16.
4:35 Infielders at "T".
Outfielders at pepper.
Pitchers and catchers work from stretch for
form, Nos. 13, 14, 16.
4:50 Bunting practice for all—catchers in full gear,
No. 176.
Introduce drag bunt, No. 177.
5:30 Pitchers at pepper.
Catchers at "T".
Outfielders fielding grounders and fly balls
and throwing.
Infielders fielding and throwing to first base-
man.

Fourth day—Thursday

4:00   Drill No. 7.
4:05   Drill No. 120.
4:10   Drill No. 116
        Catching fundamentals.
4:15   Drill No. 117.
        Catching fundamentals.
4:20   Pitcher working with first baseman on batted ball, Nos. 24, 26, 25, 27.
        Infielders, outfielders and extra catchers playing pepper and at batting "T".
4:50   Second baseman and shortstop—double play footwork, Nos. 68, 78, 122.
        Outfielders fielding flies and grounders and throwing.
        Pitchers working with catchers concentrating on form from pumping motion and stretch position, No. 17.
5:20   Bunting practice, Nos. 176, 177.
5:45   Team conditioning.

Fifth day—Friday

4:00   General warm up throwing with a few grounders.
4:10   Pitchers covering first base.
        Second basemen and shortstops practice double play, No. 122.
        Catchers and third basemen at batting "T".
        Outfielders assist where needed.
4:30   Pitcher working on stretch and throw to first base, Nos. 30, 31, 32.
        Second basemen and shortstop at batting "T".
        Outfielders and third basemen field and throw for distance.

4:50   Pitcher and catchers throwing, No. 17.
       Infielders and outfielders playing pepper.
5:15   Bunting practice, Nos. 176, 177.
5:30   Infield practice.
       Outfielders at batting "T".
5:45   Team conditioning.

Sixth day—Monday

4:00   General loosening up throwing.
4:10   Pitchers work on pick-offs at second base, Nos.
       35, 37.
       Outfielders and catchers at batting "T".
       Third basemen and first basemen playing pep-
       per.
4:25   Outfielders act as baserunners for pick-off
       practice.
       Third basemen and first basemen at batting
       "T".
4:40   Pitchers and catchers throwing, No. 17.
       Second basemen, shortstops and first basemen
       —double play, No. 122.
       Outfielders throwing alongside of gym.
5:00   Bunting practice.
5:20   Infield practice (remainder of team keep busy
       at "T" or at pepper).
5:40   Team conditioning.

Seventh day—Tuesday

4:00   General loosening up and throwing.
4:10   Bunting offensive and defensive practice, No.
       124.
       Outfielders and extra players bunt, then switch
       and allow substitutes to play.

Each pitcher pitch to about 10 batters; always
have a pitcher warming up.

5:00   Pitchers and catchers throwing, No. 17.
Infielders play pepper.
Outfielders at batting "T".

5:15   Pitchers and catchers throwing, No. 17.
Outfielders play pepper.
Infielders at batting "T".

5:30   Infield practice—outfielders, pitchers to show-
ers.
Team conditioning omitted Tuesday and
Thursday from now on.

Eighth day—Wednesday

4:00   General warm-up period.

4:10   Rundown practice using outfielders and extra
players as runners, then use replacements, No.
137.
Pitchers pick runners off base after stretch.

5:10   Pitchers throw to catchers, No. 17.
Outfielders at "T", infielders play pepper;
change after 10 minutes.

5:30   Infield practice, No. 139.
Outfielders and pitchers keep busy.

5:45   Team conditioning.

Ninth day—Thursday

4:00   General warm-up period.

4:10   Pick-off work at all bases using runners and
batters and covering all situations, No. 137.

5:10   Pitchers throw to catchers, No. 17.
Outfielders and infielders at batting "T" and
pepper.

5:30 Infield practice.
Outfielders and pitchers excused.

Tenth day—Friday

4:00 General warm-up period.
4:10 Sliding practice, No. 192.
4:40 Leads off base, Nos. 188, 189, 190, 191.
5:00 Bunting practice.
5:30 Infield practice.
5:45 Conditioning drill.

III

Outdoor Practice

THE FOLLOWING SCHEDULE ASSUMES THAT OUTDOOR drills begin two-and-a-half weeks before the first game. The drills should be geared to as near game conditions as possible, plenty of time being allowed for each situation the first time it is practiced. When players do not understand or are having difficulty executing the particular technique, it may be necessary to break the play up into several parts and progress one step at a time. This way mastery may be hastened.

Practice should start on time and finish on time. Everybody should be kept busy at all times. Practice should not be allowed to drag or become dull, each practice being an interesting experience.

If a team has not been out-of-doors previously or worked out inside, the first few days should consist of drills that will aid in conditioning, as well as reviewing and practicing fundamentals. All throwing should be at half speed and when the arm feels at all tired throwing should cease immediately. As hitting is 80 per cent of a team's offensive strength, it will represent a large share of the team's practice time and will increase as the season progresses.

The following outline is based on a two hour daily practice session with one regulation field and a small adjacent area for individual work.

First session—Monday

4:00   Announcements and talk by coach to all candidates.

4:15   Screen candidates if a large squad reports.
Pitchers and catchers playing catch and pepper.

5:45   Team calisthenics, No. 3.

6:00   Run one lap and shower.

Second session—Tuesday

4:00   Short talk by coach.

4:05   Pitchers and catchers practice Drill No. 13 for one week.
Infielders at positions, No. 128 (2 days).
Outfielders in centerfield, coach hits from foul line in right on left field, No. 104.

4:30   Pitchers on mound, covering first on ball hit to first baseman, No. 29.
Batting "T" on right field foul line.
Infielders hit outfielders fly balls.

4:50   Pitcher throwing to second baseman and shortstop after fielding ground ball, Nos. 34, 36.
Outfielders hit from "T", third basemen field balls.

5:10   Batting practice, coach pitching.
Pitcher hit balls to infielders.

5:40   Running drill, "A trip," No. 10.

6:00   Showers.

Third session—Wednesday

4:00   Talk by coach on practice plans.

4:05   Pitchers and catchers, Nos. 13, 14, 16.
Infielders, No. 128.
Outfielders fielding practice from foul line, No. 104.

4:30   Pitchers on the mound—catcher in full gear.
Infielders bunting practice, pitcher must field ball, bunter runs to first.
Outfielders at batting "T" on foul line.

4:50   Bunting practice continues, outfielders doing the bunting. Infielders at the batting "T".

5:10   Team batting practice—coach pitching.
Pitcher hits balls to infielders.

5:45   Team calisthenics, No. 3.

6:00   One lap around field and then showers.

Fourth session—Thursday

4:00   Talk by coach to squad.

4:05   Pitchers and catchers, Nos. 13, 14, 16.
Pitcher should throw to strings daily, No. 17.
Infielders at positions, normal depth and add double play.
Outfielders fielding and throwing to a cut-off man.

4:25   Pitchers on mound working on throw to first baseman.
Rundown practice between first and second—outfielders and third basemen act as runners.
Catchers on adjacent area, Nos. 46, 47, 51, 49.

4:40   Pitchers working on throw to second baseman and shortstop.
Rundown practice between second and third.
Outfielders, first basemen act as runners.

4:55 Pitcher throwing to third basemen.
      Rundown practice between third and home—
      second basemen, outfielders and first basemen
      act as runners.

5:10 Batting practice—pitchers pitching to about
      six batters apiece.
      Coach hits to infielders.

5:45 Running drill—"A trip."

6:00 Showers.

Fifth session—Friday

4:00 Talk by coach, announcing scrimmage for next
      practice.

4:05 Team bunting defense and offense.
      While pitcher is warming up, coach hits
      grounders to infielders.
      Succeeding pitchers play pepper and warm up
      for their turn.
      Substitutes and outfielders bunt and become
      base runners.
      Substitutes then take their turns in the field,
      regulars become bunters.

4:45 Batting practice; pitchers taking turns pitch-
      ing.
      Pitcher conditioner, No. 11.
      Coach hits grounders to infielders.

5:30 Infield practice.
      Outfield practice.

5:45 Team calisthenics followed by one lap.

6:00 Shower.

Sixth session—Saturday morning

9:45 Team reports and warms up.

10:00 Infield and outfield practice.

10:15   Intra-squad game.
        Pitchers go three innings followed by No. 11.
12:00   Run a lap and then showers.

Seventh session—Monday

4:00   Talk by coach commenting on intra-squad
        scrimmage practice plans and announcing final
        cut of squad after practice.
4:15   Base-running.
        1. Running to first base, No. 185.
        2. Running to second base, No. 186.
        3. Rounding all bases.
        4. Leads at first base, Nos. 187, 188.
        5. Leads at second base, No. 189.
        6. Leads at third base, No. 190.
5:00   Batting practice—five swings.
        Bunting practice: Using pitcher and catcher
        in an adjacent area; batter follows his batting
        turn by a session at bunting.
5:30   Infield practice.
        Outfield practice.
        Pitchers play pepper.
5:50   Team calisthenics.
6:00   Showers.

Eighth session—Tuesday

4:00   Talk by coach.
4:05   Pitchers loosen up and go to the mound.
        Review pitcher covering first.
        Review pitcher throwing to second baseman
        or shortstop covering second base.
4:15   Team pick-off plays.
        First without runners then add runners.

Catchers in outfield, Nos. 46, 47, 51, 49, 56.
Outfielders at batting "T".

5:00 Batting practice, pitchers doing the pitching.
Pitcher conditioner, No. 11.
Bunting practice in adjacent area.
Grounders to infielders.

5:45 Infield and outfield practice.

6:00 Run a lap and shower.

Ninth session—Wednesday

4:00 Talk by coach, announcing intra-squad game.

4:05 Bunting, offensive and defensive practice.

4:30 Intra-squad game—six innings.
Pitchers pitch nine outs in a row.
Pitchers conditioner, No. 11.

5:45 Team calisthenics.

6:00 Run one lap and shower.

Tenth session—Thursday

4:00 Coach comments on scrimmage and explains practice plans.

4:15 Base-running, Nos. 192, 193.

4:45 Batting practice.
First round No. 171, variation 10.
Second round No. 170, variation 9.
Pitcher conditioning, No. 11.

5:45 Infield and outfield practice.

6:00 Run one lap and then to showers.

Eleventh session—Friday

4:00 Coach comments on practice and announces intra-squad game plans.

4:05 All-purpose team drill, No. 194.

Pitchers play pepper if not taking turn on mound.

4:30   Catchers throwing to bases on pickoffs and steals.

5:00   All-purpose batting practice, coach pitching, No. 171.

Pitchers loosen up and play pepper.

5:45   Infield and outfield practice.

6:00   Run one lap and shower.

Twelfth session—normally Saturday morning

9:45   Team report and warm-up.

10:00   Intra-squad game.

Pitchers pitch three innings.

Pitcher conditioner, No. 11.

12:00   Run a lap and then to showers.

Thirteenth session— Monday

4:00   Coach comments on intra-squad game and plans for first league game on Wednesday.

4:05   Team bunting, defensive and offensive practice.

4:20   Team defensive practice, No. 132.

5:00   Batting practice.

First round, No. 171.

Second round, No. 169.

After turn at hitting go to bunting area.

Pitcher conditioning, No. 11.

5:45   Infield and outfield practice.

6:00   One lap and showers.

Fourteenth session—Tuesday

4:00   Coach discusses practice plans and outlines practice schedule for first game.

4:10   Pick-off practice and rundowns.
4:45   Batting practice.
       First round, No. 171.
       Second round, No. 169.
       Pitcher conditioning, No. 11.
5:30   Outfield relay practice.
5:45   Infield practice.
6:00   One lap and showers.

Fifteenth session—Wednesday—*First game*

2:15   Home team reports and warms-up.
2:30   Home team batting practice, Nos. 169, 171.
3:00   Visiting team batting practice.
3:30   Home team infield and outfield practice, No.
       139.
3:40   Visiting team infield and outfield practice.
3:50   Prepare home plate and pitchers mound for
       game.
       Umpires explain ground rules.
4:00   PLAY BALL!

Index

A

"A" trip, conditioning drill, 27-28
Advanced fielding, outfield drill, 100-110
Advancing bases, running drill, 183-184
All-around weight training, 16-20
All-purpose drills:
  base running, 184-185
  team defense, 138-139
Arm conditioning, pitcher, 31

B

Balls in dirt, catching drill, 57-58
Base running drills, 169-175
  advancing, 183-184
  all-purpose, 184-185
  competitive season, during, 186
  determining leads, 178-179
  indoors practice, pre-season, 176-182
  leading off base:
    second, 180-181
    third, 181
  outdoors practice, pre - season, 182-186

Base running drills (*cont.*):
  returning to base:
    first, 179-180
    second, 180-181
  running:
    to first, 177-178
    practice, 176-177
    to second, 182-183
    starting, 176-177
  sliding practice, 185-186
Bat control, 148-149
Batting drills:
  breaking-the-wrist, 151
  bat control, 148-149
  competitive season, during, 167-168
  developing hitters, 161-162
  early season, 160-161
  faulty stride, correcting, 161, 162
  follow through, 150-151
  gaining confidence, 163
  hip-swing, 154-155
    with dumbells, 154-155
  indoors practice, pre-season, 148-159
  "Looking them over . . . ," 158-159